D1248130

How to Market Professional Services

How to Market Professional Services

Bernard Katz

Nichols Publishing Company
New York

© Bernard Katz, 1988

First published in the United States of America in 1988 by Nichols Publishing Company,
Post Office Box 96
New York, N.Y. 10024

Library of Congress Cataloging-in-Publication Data

Katz, Bernard,
  How to market professional services.
  Bibliography: p.
  1. Professions——Marketing. I. Title
HD8038.A1K37   1988   658.8   88–12587

ISBN 0–89397–322–X

Printed in Great Britain

Contents

PART II   THE SKILLS OF MARKETING

Illustrations

Tables

Preface

The marketing of professional services is a relatively new concept. It is enthusiastically adopted by some; for others, professional excellence is the only pathway for practice development.

But marketing is not in conflict with the dignity of the professions. This book provides marketing skills designed to complement organic practice growth. It is in two parts: Part I deals with strategic marketing, the planning process which determines the directions the firm should take. 'Where are we now?' and 'Where do we want to go?' are questions to be asked and answered in this stage.

Part II presents specific skills. Negotiating, selling and making a presentation are marketing skills. In many cases practitioners have not found the time or the opportunity to bring the level of these skills up to those of

their professional discipline. Checklists, examples, and
rules for what to do and what to avoid are therefore
provided. They allow readers to apply those techniques
and tactics most likely to enhance practice progress.
Detailed guidance on training is offered as well. In-house
training sessions can reinforce the process whereby all
in the firm adopt the marketing function, particularly
where this represents change.

Through the book a question-and-answer format is
used. A short list of 'test' questions precedes each
chapter. These questions are then worked through in the
text. The same questions, together with answers, appear
at the end of each chapter as a summary. In some cases,
when consistent with the subject material, the questions
are open-ended. Such questions are not really a 'test':
the reader's answer may differ from the one given, but
it is not necessarily wrong. The objective of the question-
and-answer format is to highlight specific practice development problems and issues resolved through a
marketing approach.

My warmest thanks go to Martin Iles, sometime
lecturing colleague, for sharing his knowledge and
experience of the practice of architecture. I am aware of
a debt, too, to the practitioners I meet in the classroom.
More than a few have confessed, at the end of marketing
courses, their initial doubts about the contribution
marketing can make to their marketing progress.

Bernard Katz

PART I
Strategic Marketing

1 Marketing professional services

Before reading this chapter try to answer the following questions. The material is worked through in the text. Questions and answers appear together at the end of the chapter by way of summary.

QUESTIONS

What is the marketing function?

What are the arguments in favour of a professional practice adopting the marketing function?

What are the arguments against professional firms adopting the marketing function?

What are the variables known as the 'marketing mix'?

What forces in the marketplace for professional services are beyond control?

What might be the terms of reference for the professional company adopting the marketing function?

Chapter 1 synopsis
- A definition
- The advantages marketing brings
- Caution
- How is it done?
- Uncontrollable variables
- A structure for success

A DEFINITION

Question What is the marketing function?

First, an explanation. Marketing is a recent concept; it is a positive approach to increasing profits. Marketing was formulated and practised in the struggle for growth and rebuilding, following the Second World War. Marketing in its earliest form applies to manufactured products – baked beans are marketed, soap is marketed. In popular thought, marketing is another way of talking about advertising.

Marketing concentrates on clients, the client is No. 1. But it was not always like this. Marketing has evolved in the commercial marketplace, where goods are traded and sold – with a capital 'S'. The manufacturer designs the product he thinks the customer can use, which is then sold aggressively. If one customer does not buy, another is found.

Big business becomes a battle between the strongest manufacturers and traders. The more goods that are sold, the stronger is the pressure on suppliers to reduce the price of product components and raw materials. In this way the price to the consumer is reduced so that even more goods are sold.

Nonetheless, some products die off. Either the product reaches the end of its projected life cycle or it is overtaken by more effective competition. So the manufacturer compensates by having more products. Bigger and better products – and lots of them – create a product concept: products with a capital 'P'. If one product does not sell, another gains the order. Manufacturers strive to find even greater profitability.

Meanwhile, professional practices behave as they have always behaved. Architects are given commissions because they are good at architecture; solicitors are consulted because they have acted previously for a person or company known to the client.

In the marketplace in the late 1940s it became apparent that the demand for 'what the customer really needs' is virtually unlimited. But it has to be the true 'need': what a manufacturer, or supplier of a service, thinks a customer ought to need is not the same.

Marketing is identifying client needs, satisfying them – and earning profits. So a working definition of the marketing function incorporates those three aspects:

- identifying the needs of buyers and potential buyers in their market segments;
- satisfying those needs by selling the appropriate service or product;
- making a profit.

The marketing function is a discipline that enables 'marketing' to take place. Of necessity the marketing function is structured (see Figure 1.1 'The marketing approach').

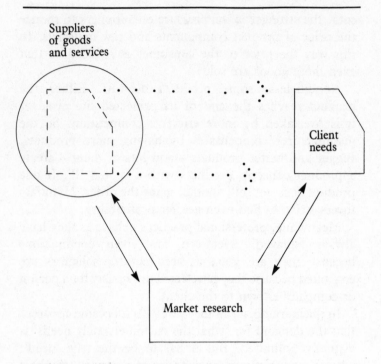

Figure 1.1   The marketing approach

Information gathering Through research, new and existing data are collected, classified and stored. The data are pertinent to the profession or industry, for example the incidence of cardiac arrest in a county over the last three years, or the number of trumpets imported from China in the preceding year.

This material is subsequently used for decision-making in respect of the services or products to be supplied, or a market segment to be targeted.

Identification of client needs The precise needs and requirements of clients are found, thus making possible the full satisfaction of those needs. Prior to this awareness through marketing of what clients really wanted, products and services often gave only partial satisfaction. This was accepted by the clients because there were no alternative options.

Clients and customers are categorized into groups known as 'market segments'. Within any segment all share similar needs. Property developers form a segment – with a need for land on which to build. Children needing spectacles are another segment; so are actors requiring cosmetic dentistry.

Supply of goods and services There are many sub-functions. The services or goods are designed to match consumer needs as closely as possible, based on the information available through market research. But success is equally a function of the resources of the firm or organization. An exact match of the consumer need to the product or service offered will not guarantee that the consumer accepts the offer. Services and products have to be promoted and sold, they must be made available for the consumer to consider and select. And there is competition from other sources which are trying to provide their services or products to the consumer.

Monitoring the effectiveness of the supply of services and goods Ongoing feedback is required from the marketplace. Are client needs being satisfied fully? Research of markets and marketing is an essential tool of the marketing function. Bedrock questions in marketing are 'What profession am I in?' or 'What business am I in?' The marketplace is not static: dynamic forces create change – often not seen by those involved in the change. For example, what are the problems faced by the modern dentist? The teeth of the modern child often need little or no work. This is a totally different perspective from that faced by the dentist's father in his practice. Is the situation the same now for a dentist as it was last year, or five or ten years ago?

Another example is taken from industry. In the North of England a self-made millionaire consigned his heirs to everlasting poverty. He had amassed his fortune from the manufacture and sale of mechanical calculators. He wrote in his will that the shares in his company must never be sold, because 'there will always be a demand in industry for the reliability of mechanical calculators'. Shortly after his death the advent of electronic calculation, and the microchip, brought about the demise of his company. The manufacturer thought he was in the business of manufacturing mechanical calculators – really he was in the business of helping people to count.

THE ADVANTAGES MARKETING BRINGS

Question   What are the arguments in favour of a professional practice adopting the marketing function?

There are pros and cons to a professional practice adopting the marketing function. Marketing is not simply having the word 'Marketing' painted on an office door. Nor is it sufficient for an employee to be designated 'marketing manager'.

Marketing is a philosophy orientated towards putting clients and their needs and wants first. In a professional practice which markets its services, the marketing momentum is initiated by the principal or partners. It then permeates downwards to all personnel. The results of marketing are achieved through the application of marketing strategies employing diverse marketing tactics and techniques. The arguments in favour of adopting a marketing approach are few in number, but they are very strong:

Traditional markets are being eroded Take health care for example: advances in technology, increasing use of preventive medicine and dentistry, psychotherapy, generally increased sophistication and skill, all contribute to the shrinking of long-established demand.

In professions such as architecture, engineering, planning and surveying, international business is closely tied to an external factor – world demand for oil. A slump in the oil industry has a knock-on effect on the professions. When the number of clients and the volume of client needs reduce, competition becomes fierce for such business as does exist.

In a number of professions some practices already adopt the marketing function Marketing is currently the most effective approach to generating new business. When a client base is strong, and external factors do not impinge too heavily, traditional patterns continue. Business is placed with the professional advisers and consultants just as it used to be placed. But securing instructions from new quarters can be a different story. The firm or partnership has to make sure that it is selected in competition with many others. Being seen to be competent, creative and professionally capable is an image avidly sought through marketing tactics.

Client expectations are changing Adherents to the mystique of the professional person as omniscient are decreasing. Potential clients seek to know the background and track record of the firm or partnership they are considering approaching. They seek guarantees of levels of skill. Currently it is commonplace for members of the public to telephone firms of solicitors asking the fee for conveyancing or other professional work. Such calls were unheard of a few years ago.

CAUTION

Question   What are the arguments against professional firms adopting the marketing function?

Partners in traditional, well-established professional firms do not all subscribe to an involvement in marketing. The following opinions reflect the attitudes of those who have found, or strive for, success in professional excellence.

Marketing tactics are not compatible with the dignity of a profession   For many people marketing suggests high-pressure 'American' tactics applied to consumer goods. The tactics that are brash, and right for promoting soap and baked beans, are not the tactics with which the professions can associate.

There are few persuasive arguments for a profession to debase itself. If marketing diminishes the level of professional service clearly it must be rejected. Proponents of marketing, on the other hand, argue that marketing makes use of proven activities from a highly developed field of communication and creative effort.

The professional person is trained in professional skills. He or she is not equipped to practise marketing   Marketing is itself a skill. Without the training to initiate and implement the marketing function, random marketing activities have little likelihood of success. Marketing activities – research, planning, promoting, distributing, selling, pricing – are not themselves difficult. But they must be designed and initiated, for others in the practice to implement. For this reason there are strong arguments for professional firms to consult or employ professional marketing personnel.

In commercial companies the marketing director/

manager works closely with the managing director. The marketing role has usurped that of the sales function. As a general rule sales managers now report to the marketing managers.

HOW IS IT DONE?

Question **What are the variables known as the 'marketing mix'?**

In the marketplace many forces are at work: some are in the control of the marketer, others not. The variables that are controllable are known as the 'marketing mix'. These variables – product, price, place, promotion and service – are known as 'the four Ps and an S'.

Figure 1.2 shows the marketing mix in diagrammatic form. The starting point is client needs. 'Client needs' is a generic term covering all the needs that buyers have – from eye testing to loft conversion, to learning how to play the harpsichord. Needs are differentiated into the categories known as 'market segments' – within a segment all the buyers and potential buyers have identical needs.

Market research diagrammatically links the four Ps and an S. It is the prime tool for data collection, on which marketing decisions are subsequently based. Research quantifies and qualifies the nature of client needs, and it monitors the effectiveness of the process of satisfying those needs. Whenever it is found from the research that needs are not totally satisfied, the marketer develops and produces the right 'product' and/or service to meet the demand.

Figure 1.2   Controllable factors of the marketing mix: four Ps and an S

Product

For the professional organization product is the total package of professional skills that is delivered to the client. For example, product is an appendectomy, a transport infrastructure for a new town or a church wedding service. For the commercial organization product is a crate of plums, a piano or an aeroplane.

Product for the professional organization, though often a basket of highly specialized service skills, is distinguished from the 'service' of the marketing mix. Service is the peripheral effort from the supplier of the product to the client or customer. In many cases it is an important feature of the client's decision to purchase. If the client is not convinced that the capacity for service is adequate to meet contingent demands, he or she is not persuaded to a purchase.

Products have a life cycle. Figure 1.3 illustrates the stages of the product life cycle – launch, growth, maturity and decline. When, say, falling fee income indicates that the product is in its decline stage, a second peak is sometimes achieved by means of vigorous promotion. This is illustrated in Figure 1.4.

Take, for example, an architectural draughtsman who designs and produces building drawings for home extensions, in his local borough. By word of mouth, and from regular classified advertisements in the local press, the volume of instructions increases to a satisfactory level. A down-turn in building due to increased loan interest rates causes the draughtsman's business to shrink. Increased promotional effort by direct mail, advertisement in additional media, and PR literature at clubs, halls and local society activities, produces a larger share of that existing business which is itself diminishing.

Price

Getting the pricing right results from knowing what goes on at the place where the services are sold. That is the starting point for research. There are a number of interacting factors:

- whether fee levels mean status or value to the client;
- competitor pricing;
- objectives of the company providing the service;
- whether profitability is more important than market penetration;
- whether fee levels are designed to pre-empt competitor strategies;

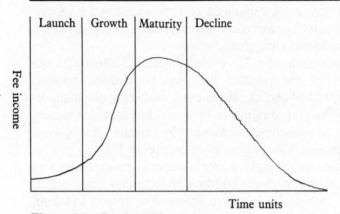

Figure 1.3   Product life cycle

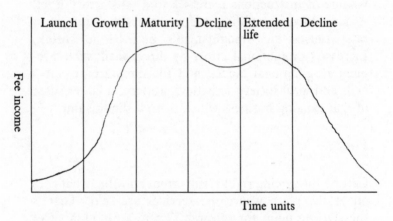

Figure 1.4   Extended product life cycle

- margins of profit necessary to certain distribution channels;
- capacity to supply professional services.

It is incumbent on the seller of a product or service to check that the price is the best one attainable. Just because a buyer buys at price X does not mean to say that he would not buy at X +1 or X +2. If the pricing is wrong, there is no one to scold the seller. It simply means that profits are lower than they need be.

Place

'Place' describes the outlets through which services are offered to users. In many cases there is a direct sale by the service supplier to the user, but there are situations where intermediaries are used. For example, the house purchaser makes contact directly with a solicitor; or is recommended to the solicitor by the estate agent.

Direct sale provides much better control over how the service is given, and how it is received. The feedback that is possible is important because changing needs can require amended service. It is also easier to reinforce the image of service differentiation from that supplied by competitors. But there are constraints to direct sale: geographical barriers can intervene in the contact between provider and client; there are limitations to the workload capacity of the single service supplier, for example a sculptor or a medical specialist.

The range of intermediaries in the offering of service is rather wide.

- Agents. They work purely on the basis of commission, offering services such as finance, insurance or industrial processes.
- Brokers. Their function is similar to that of an agent. The code of practice is more precisely defined. Examples are the stock market and insurance.
- Dealers. A form of subcontract from the principal supplier of the service. Dealers themselves act as principals in the transactions.
- Retailers. An example is pharmacy.

Promotion

Promotion is the 'how' of bringing awareness of the
service to the service user. It is also the 'how' of making
the buyer buy. Promotional activities include advertising, word of mouth, PR, sponsorship and personal
selling. Many professions impose a strict code of conduct
upon promotional activities, jealously guarding and
sustaining an image of propriety and respectability.

Service

Service is the spectrum of activities which enhance the
client's expectation and enjoyment of the 'Product'
benefits. A dentist may be good at his or her dentistry
– it is the core service – but this is not the sole consideration. The efficiency of the appointments system; the
availability of dental service out of hours for emergency
treatment; and the degree of comfort of the waiting room
are all service factors – peripheral service. At conscious
and unconscious levels peripheral service influences the
decision to consult with any particular dentist.

UNCONTROLLABLE VARIABLES

Question **What forces in the marketplace for
professional services are beyond control?**

Irrespective of the level of skill of the service provided,
there are some external forces exerting independent
influence – they cannot be controlled. These forces are
illustrated in Figure 1.5.

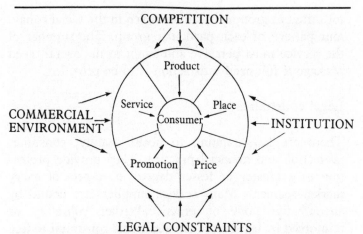

Figure 1.5 Controllable and uncontrollable variables of the marketing mix

Competition

The supplier of the service cannot directly control the strategies and tactics of the competition. He can predict them, he can react to them – even pre-empt anticipated actions; but that is all. Because the competition is beyond control it is important that data on competitive activities, successes and abuses are regularly monitored.

Commercial environment

Lifestyles differ, social and family codes are diverse; and so are the ways in which many consumers must by tradition purchase their services. The legal profession, for example, jealously guards the distinctive roles of solicitor and barrister. The one does not advise in the other's field, even if there is common expertise.

The cultural environment is an equally significant factor where clients come from different ethnic and national groups. Whilst the basic need may be identical for different groups, it is interwoven in the social behaviour pattern of each particular group. The supplier of the service must perceive and adapt to the overall need package if full need satisfaction is to be provided.

Legal constraints

There are laws relating to health, safety, consumer protection and financial practice. They provide protection to a greater or lesser degree in respect of every market segment. Many service suppliers are bound by an effective code of practice, either voluntary or reinforced by legislation. An additional constraint to free marketing is that practitioners of professional services must qualify by passing recognized examinations.

Institutions

Institutions in this context are those professional and public organizations which reflect awareness and support of the rights of the client. If a consumer is aggrieved, alleging infringement of an individual or public right, action can be taken on his or her behalf. For example, the Advertising Standards Authority has the power to cause the withdrawal of advertisement copy upheld as offensive, racist or prejudicial.

A STRUCTURE FOR SUCCESS

Question   **What might be the terms of reference for a professional company adopting the marketing function?**

Marketing is a philosophy. It is a framework of attitudes directed towards clients and their needs. But there are parameters within which the marketing activities function. These are set by defining terms of reference. Likely terms of reference include the following.

The public image   The image of the professional firm is seen by many parties. The images are not necessarily the same, but the firm may not know that they are different. A good public image is not automatic or guaranteed, neither is it constant. Every person in the firm who has direct or indirect contact with the public makes a contribution to that image.

Competition   There is always increasing competition and competitiveness. For example, in the architectural profession there are currently stringent pressures in the private sector. These arise from computer-aided design systems, from other firms and from end-users seeking a reduction in price and an increase in the service, with exacting demands for performance on time, to budget and to specification.

The profession's trade cycle   The stage of the cycle for the profession as a whole is important. Equally significant is the position of the firm's specialism. What opportunities for growth remain with the present service path?

The home market   The special needs of the domestic market, in terms of labour, capital and the application of technology, must be identified. Reference to the historical background of the firm is necessary, as this is an important influence on development within the market.

Overseas markets   In which markets are there least constraints? Language, client attitudes, local practice, clients' ability to pay and geographical distance are all inherent problems in exporting professional services.

Alternative market sectors Sectors of a market are gross divisions permitting targeting over a broad spectrum. For example, the economy is divisible into private and public sectors; sectors are further divisible into segments.

New market segments The progressive firm must seek to develop activities within new segments. Criteria can be those permitting fee rates which give an acceptable profit return on capital employed.

Territories Specialization is by territory, service, experience, sophistication or technological orientation. Territory commands serious consideration for its direct relationship to the effectiveness of service supply.

Pricing strategies There is a range of options from marginal costing to premium pricing.

Fee rates Are fee rates depressed in comparison with other professions? Fees must reflect the calibre of the service supplied.

Trends in the marketplace The needs and the attitudes of clients change. External forces distort traditional opportunities and practice. Trends must be identified and recorded on a regular basis.

Profitability Earnings and costs are analysed to identify the profit contribution from each profit centre. With or without the marketing function, a precise awareness of all costs is the bedrock of survival. Profitability stems largely from the management of costs.

Pathways to growth Growth and diversification are parallel activities. They fall into four categories:

- present services in present markets;
- new services for existing markets;
- new markets for existing services;
- new services in new markets.

Strategic planning There are three questions to be asked:

- Where is the firm now?
- Where is it to go?
- Where will it go without marketing direction?

The historical growth pattern of the firm is analysed in relation to current and long-term objectives.

Strengths and weaknesses Strengths and weaknesses impose limits on performance and achievement. Marketing tactics can be designed to strengthen, to eliminate weakness, and to build on strengths exploiting them to the full.

Risk factor Political, financial and commerical risks exist. Forecasting and planning allow services, territories and clients to be grouped into priority market segments. In this way short, medium and long-term objectives are met.

The marketing package The marketing mix ensures that appropriate skills, techniques and price are matched as closely as possible to the market segment needs.

SUMMARY

Question **What is the marketing function?**

Answer The marketing function has three aspects:

- identifying the needs of buyers and potential buyers in their market segments;
- satisfying those needs by selling the appropriate service or product;
- making a profit.

Question **What are the arguments in favour of a professional practice adopting the marketing function?**

Answer the arguments in favour of a marketing approach are few but very strong:

- traditional markets are being eroded;
- in a number of professions some practices already adopt the marketing function;
- client expectations are changing.

Question **What are the arguments against professional firms adopting the marketing function?**

Answer Reasons given to reject the marketing function are:

- marketing tactics are not compatible with the dignity of a profession;
- the professional person is trained in professional skills. He or she is not equipped to practise marketing.

Question **What are the variables known as the 'marketing mix'?**

Answer   The variables controlled by the marketer, known as the marketing mix, are – product, price, place, promotion and service. They are known as four Ps and an S.

Question   What forces in the marketplace for professional services are beyond control?

Answer   There are certain external forces in the marketplace over which control can never be gained. They are competition, commercial environment, legal constraints and institutions.

Question   What might be the terms of reference for a professional company adopting the marketing function?

Answer   the terms of reference provide the parameters within which marketing activities function. The terms of reference are: the public image; competition; the profession's trade cycle; the home market; overseas markets; alternative market sectors; new market segments; territories; pricing strategies; fee rates; trends in the marketplace; profitability; pathways to growth; strategic planning; strengths and weaknesses; risk factor; the marketing package.

2 Researching current and potential markets

Before reading this chapter try to answer the following questions. The material is worked through in the text. Questions and answers appear together at the end of the chapter by way of summary.

QUESTIONS

What is the context of market research?

What types of data does a researcher collect?

What are the two basic procedures of market research?

What research is appropriate to a professional practice seeking to develop the scope of its activities?

What practical step is helpful to a practitioner commencing his or her own research activities?

What major external forces in the marketplace influence current and potential customer needs?

What is the activity that shares social and research benefits?

Chapter 2 synopsis

- How market research helps
- The range of research data
- How research is carried out
- Findings
- How to begin
- External market forces
- Networking

HOW MARKET RESEARCH HELPS

Question **What is the context of market research?**

Market research is the starting point for expansion. It is also the activity which launches a programme for survival. To borrow from the definition of the American Marketing Association, market research is the systematic gathering, recording and analysing of data about problems relating to the marketing of goods and services. There are two basic functions of market research:

- to reduce the uncertainties of the decision-making process of marketing;
- to monitor and control the performance of marketing activities.

In marketing terms, market research is a discipline available for use and application by the one-man practitioner and by the large organization alike. There are eight discrete stages.

Definition of the problem Examples are: how can fee income be increased? What opportunities are there for international business development?

Finding a solution Market research is never a total solution: it is the foundation stone on which solutions are built. It is necessary to identify how market research can help.

Aims and objectives Aims are where one wants to go. Objectives define how those aims are to be achieved and must necessarily be precise and quantifiable. In this way subsequent performance is measurable.

Terms of reference Parameters are set within which research is to be carried out.

Research data are collected A structured approach is the most productive. Details are given below.

Analysis, interpretation and yield Statistical formulae permit the reliability of quantified data to be established.

Research report, conclusions and recommendations Reports prepared for decision-making by others should be presented in a precise professional format. A summary is valuable so that the reader learns immediately what has taken place, what has been achieved and what it is possible to achieve in terms of the recommendations of the researcher.

Marketing decisions are made.

THE RANGE OF RESEARCH DATA

Question **What types of data does a researcher collect?**

Two types of information exist.

Secondary information This already exists and is published or recorded in some form or other: for example, the number of veterinary surgeons practising in Derbyshire. The information can be extracted from Yellow Pages. It is also available from the profession's Year Book.

Primary information Ad hoc information is newly created. It is collected specifically for the purpose of meeting set objectives, for example a comparison of average treatment times for rural and urban practitioners.

   The information is gathered by questioning a statistically reliable sample of veterinary practices.

HOW RESEARCH IS CARRIED OUT

Question **What are the two basic procedures of market research?**

Figure 2.1 illustrates the procedures of market research. They are secondary research and primary (or field) research.

Secondary research

Secondary research is subdivided into two areas.

Procedures in

MARKET RESEARCH

■ **1. Internal Audit**

Secondary Research

■ **2. Desk Research**

Primary Research

■ **3. Field Research**

Figure 2.1   The procedures of market research

Internal Audit   Data and information are taken from existing records within the company or practice. The information is unlikely to be neatly packaged and labelled in a way that is helpful to the researcher on his or her current assignment. But information often exists, relating to past professional activities, successes, failures, obstacles, researches or client behaviour, which has a bearing on the present research.

Desk research   Desk research is a generic term, covering all research that is not 'field research' seeking primary information. Desk research often encompasses visits to professional organization libraries, chambers of commerce, university research organizations, data banks and so on. Overseas desk research – even though it involves an element of travel – is classified as desk research, if only published and printed secondary information is sought.

In addition to data from traditional sources, valuable information is also obtainable through computer-linked data transmission systems. Prestel is one such system, Viewdata is another. Access is not expensive. Entry to the system is through a microcomputer via a modem and the public telephone network. Thousands of pages of classified data and information are available at low cost. Prestel charges a fee on a time basis for the information taken, plus the traditional telephone line costs. Information supplied is stored on micro-computer disc.

When carrying out desk research, it is important to know where to go to look for information. The following checklist gives the most important sources of information.

Checklist: Basic sources of information

- Professional institutes
- Chambers of commerce
- University research organizations
- Libraries
- Competitive practitioners
- Commercial market research organizations
- Personal contacts
- Exhibitions
- Banks

The second checklist gives the most important printed sources of information.

Checklist: Major printed sources of information

- Professional journals and publications
- Trade press

- Published surveys
- Government publications
- HM Customs and Excise statistics
- Confederation of British Industry
- Prestel
- Credit agencies
- Academic and scientific publications
- International statistical publications
- Competitor literature

It is not practical to list more than a few examples of printed sources. Knowing where to go is what counts. An excellent starting point is with two of the publications sponsored by the Department of Trade and Industry:

- *The International Directory of Published Market Research*;
- *The International Directory of Market Research Organizations.*

Field research

Field research often is referred to as *ad hoc* or primary research. Material is collected by observation, face-to-face interview, letter, telephone, telex or through audio-visual recording. Structured questionnaires, carefully avoiding weighted and leading questions, can probe to extract pertinent research data.

Field research falls into five main areas.

1   *Distribution research*

Information is sought on the following.

Existing channel structures   How services are provided to the end-user.

Potential channel structures   Agents or organizations able to provide services remote from the source. An example would be a London surveyor arranging for a client's house in Glasgow to be surveyed.

Channel margins and fees   What are the traditional fees? What scale do competitive service suppliers give to the middlemen in the channels?

2   Service research

Concept testing   Are the idea of the service and its benefits acceptable?

Attitude testing   How does the marketplace see the service? Do preformed hostile attitudes exist?

Client profiles   Who are the users of the service? What are their needs, their lifestyles, their behaviour patterns, their disposable incomes?

Health requirements   What conditions and what constraints must be met for the service to be acceptable.

Legal requirements   What conditions and what constraints prescribed by law can diminish or enhance the supply of services?

Client loyalty   How much marketing effort is necessary to sustain and increase client support?

3   Service format research

Level of sophistication   How fully does the supply of the service match client needs? Is there saturation or a shortfall?

Regional variation What correlations exist with geographic/demographic variables?

Service packages What options exist to tie diverse service supply to a single package?

Education and training How effective is existing supply? What changes can be productive?

4 Advertising research

Advertising research is most effectively carried out by the specialist departments of the larger advertising agencies. Sophisticated techniques are usually employed, including mathematical modelling.

Copy testing Within the context of professional standards and ethics what wording has the greatest impact?

Media coverage This information is available from all media owners in published form.

Media effectiveness Literacy, ownership of television and radio receivers and regional coverage are all important for decision-making.

Campaign costs How is cost-effectiveness to be evaluated?

5 Pricing research

Service demand elasticity What effect on demand is achieved through price variation?

Competitive pricing What parameters are set by other suppliers of service?

Fee costs analysis   What fixed costs are common? Which factors influence variable costs contributions?

FINDINGS

Question   What research is appropriate to a professional practice seeking to develop the scope of its activities?

Market research campaigns are designed with the yield in mind. It is from the yield that conclusions leading to decision-making are formulated. If the information is not available as secondary information, it is gained from interviews with end-users, with channel middlemen when they exist, and with practitioners.

The following information is important.

- The current market in terms of value and consultations.
- The future market: the likely growth prospects expressed in value/volume terms.
- The market structure: a description of the range of salient segments. The relative importance of direct selling to middlemen.
- User attitudes and purchasing practice. What are:
  - the levels of satisfaction with existing services?
  - the degree of service back-up support provided?
  - the perceived strengths and weaknesses of suppliers of service in the market?
  - existing/latent demand for improvements to services which are currently available?
  - opportunities for piggy-back marketing of ancillary services?
  - preferred pricing levels/terms of payment?
  - the decision-making processes in the selection of service and service supplier?

HOW TO BEGIN

Question **What practical step is helpful to a practitioner commencing his or her own research activities?**

The starting point for desk research is the internal audit. A practical step therefore is the design of a service mix audit grid to identify the utilization of skills resources and their profitability.

Questions to ask are: What is the situation now? What was the situation X years ago? How do clients perceive the service now? How have client attitudes changed? Are there ambivalent attitudes as, for example in dentistry, where the image of the dentist may be poor but the image of the benefit received from dentistry high?

Figure 2.2 shows a service mix audit grid prepared for an architectural practice. The analysis is segmented by building type to identify:

- the percentage of fee income derived from each segment activity;
- the percentage of professional capacity utilized to satisfy that segment;
- an evaluation of the service demand trend on a three-point scale of low/static/high;
- potential services which could be offered, matched against known service demand trends.

When completed the service mix audit grid is a precise quantified document. Other questions can be asked to complement the findings of the grid. There follows an internal audit checklist to structure the research.

Internal audit checklist

- Are the fees adequate for the services provided?
- Why do clients select our service against the competition?

EXISTING SERVICES AND DISCIPLINES

(by building type)	% of fee income	% of professional skill capacity utilized	Service demand trend		
			Low	Static	High
HOSPITALS					
Teaching	21	9		•	
General	7	10		•	
Specialist	19	23			•
Private	12	18			•
INSTITUTIONAL AND ACADEMIC					
Universities	8	7		•	
Colleges Poly.	4	5		•	
Second. Edu.	6	5		•	
Specialist	7	5			•
Museums	1	3	•		
Libraries	2	4	•		
Civic	1	4	•		
Other	4	4	•		
OTHER	8	3	•		
POTENTIAL SERVICES Potential Fee Income %					
Interiors					•
Graphics				•	
Struct. Eng.					•
Civil Eng.			•		
Landscape Arch.					•
Product Design			•		
Project Manage.					•
Cost Consultant					•
Surveying				•	

Figure 2.2   Service mix audit grid

- Why does the public buy competitive services?
- What information on competitor activities do I regularly record?
- How does the public know of our services?
- What additional promotional activities could be employed?
- What image do our clients have of our services?
- What role does marketing play in generating new business?

- What involvement does the total practice have in the marketing function?
- What future growth is likely without involvement in marketing?
- What are the firm's strengths?
- What are the weaknesses?

EXTERNAL MARKET FORCES

Question **What major external forces in the marketplace influence current and potential customer needs?**

The objectives of market research for a professional firm are set to identify and demarcate the forces in the marketplace. There are a number of forces which are common to different companies within a profession. The following checklists offer a basis for probing each of the variables. For real-life research each checklist can be enlarged and customized to meet specific needs.

Checklist for competition

- What degree of specialization is offered by competitors?
- What market share do suppliers of competitive services have?
- What is the technology skills basis for competitor strengths?
- What is the resource basis for competitor strengths?
- What market research is known to be carried out by competitors?
- What channels of distribution are used by competitors?
- What remuneration package is paid to agents?

- Can competitors' agents be recruited?
- How are the services of successful competitors marketed?
- What are competitors' income, credit and discount terms?
- How do the services of successful competitors differ from our own?
- What trends are likely to reduce competition?
- In which service segments is there least competition?
- What changes in the profession's infrastructure are projected?

Checklist for cultural environment

- What are the profiles of the clients in their different client segments?
- Does the supply of 'traditional' or 'standard' service fully satisfy client needs?
- How do clients perceive the services provided?
- How do we want clients to perceive the services provided?
- Are special support services appropriate to the principal service supplied?
- Are the lifestyle, business practice and ethics of ethnic clients known?

Checklist for legal environment

- What legislation exists for health/safety/financial control?
- What government aid schemes exist – for training, research, marketing, design, development, exports and so on?
- What changes in legislation are likely in the short term and in the medium term?

- Is the firm ready to take advantage of change immediately it is introduced?
- For what other change should a professional lobby be supported/instigated?
- How have competitive firms taken advantage of recent changes in the law or in the ethical guidelines for professional behaviour?

Checklist for institutions

- What consumer movements have taken issue with professional malpractice?
- What professional body external to the profession monitors professional standards?
- How does the public measure professional competence?
- What recourse do aggrieved clients have for alleged malpractice?

NETWORKING

Question   What is the activity that shares social and research benefits?

Networking is a valuable marketing technique. It entails establishing professional and business contacts to provide information and referrals that result in work. When a firm's principal is very active in professional, community or social affairs, networking happens almost by accident. Network contacts also spin off from the practice-development energies of the founder of a professional firm. A network example for an architectural practice is illustrated in Figure 2.3.

Creating and monitoring a network are considered by some to have more dignity than the overt selling of professional services. Overt selling is essentially one-

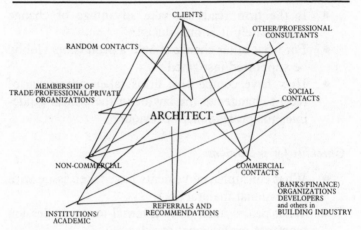

Figure 2.3 Network of contacts for an architectural practice

sided, at least at the beginning of the relationship. A network relationship is essentially one of mutual interest – both parties expect to receive a benefit, and an ongoing transfer of business cements and reinforces the relationship. Clearly those who contribute more to a relationship benefit in the long term; those who set out to exploit a network rarely get the same return.

Five essential ingredients help to maintain an effective network.

Listing Listing identifies individuals likely to have information that can be used by the firm or to have use for information that may be known to the firm. Individuals might be other consultants, contractors, estate agents, bankers, accountants, solicitors or public officials. A network of fifteen to twenty-five key contacts is generally sufficient for one individual to service.

Helpfulness The objective of networking is helpfulness, so it is important constantly to be alert for information which might be of value to one or more members of the network. The value of information is often time-related. It is important to let network contacts know within twenty-four hours.

Updating The network should be kept aware of the firm's progress. There is then a basis for identifying whatever is of value. It should never be assumed that others know of new developments if they have not been specifically told – even where there is media publicity.

Asking for help Provided the relationship is reciprocal – based on mutual exchange – it is always possible to ask for specific help.

Networking is status-free Networks are created at all levels, regardless of status or title. People do tend to work best with those of like age. It is therefore possible to maintain several networks within a firm at the same time.

SUMMARY

Question **What is the context of market research?**

Answer Market research is the bedrock of both survival and expansion. It is the process of information gathering providing a basis for marketing decision-making.

Question **What types of data does a researcher collect?**

Answer There are two types of information:

- Secondary information is data published or recorded somewhere.

- Primary information is data specifically gathered for a particular purpose.

Question **What are the basic procedures of market research?**

Answer The prime activities of market research are desk research and field research. The former seeks to identify existing and published research facts available from records, publications and computer databases.

Field research is concerned with finding new, previously unrecorded specific data – by observation or through analysis of non-specific published data.

Question **What research is appropriate to a professional practice seeking to develop the scope of its activities?**

Answer The information sought relates to historical, current and future market activities. It should also disclose market structure, client profiles and approach to decision-making, and the strengths and weaknesses of competitors.

Question **What practical step is helpful to a practitioner commencing his or her own research activities?**

Answer The starting point for a research project is an internal audit of historical practice performance. Checklists should be prepared in advance to ensure that probing questions are able to disclose pertinent data.

Question **What major external forces in the market place influence current and potential client needs?**

Answer Major influences on current and potential

client needs are competitors and the professions' institutes.

Question   **What is the activity that shares social and research benefits?**

Answer   A network of contacts developed with peers engaged in peripheral and contingent activities has considerable benefit – provided that the basis of the relationship is reciprocal. Social relationships reinforce the mutual exchange of professional information, advice and help.

3   Developing new business

Before reading this chapter try to answer the following questions. The material is worked through in the text. Questions and answers appear together at the end of the chapter by way of summary.

QUESTIONS

What is the business development path for the professional firm in a changing marketplace?

What information is needed by management in the analysis stage of a business development programme?

What are the fundamental questions to be asked in setting development objectives?

What are the essential marketing ingredients of an action plan?

What does control mean in marketing terms?

Chapter 3 synopsis

- The way to go
- The information needed
- Basics
- How to get there
- The importance of control

THE WAY TO GO

Question **What is the business development path for the professional firm in a changing marketplace?**

When the marketplace is static, business continues between existing practices and clients. But it does not grow. Growth happens when needs change and expand. Growth also follows when different needs from other sources are identified and satisfied.

Business development is a multi-stage process. It is illustrated in Figure 3.1.

Analysis

Analysis is the process of identifying the current position. What are the available resources? What are the professional skills available? What is the firm's position in the marketplace? Who are the clients and potential clients? What are the needs of those clients? What external forces intrude?

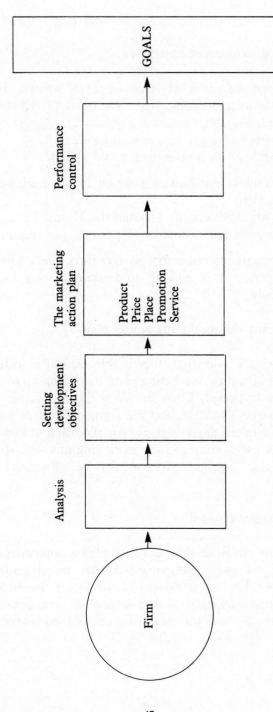

Figure 3.1 The business development path

Setting development objectives

This stage defines what achievement is wanted. It is setting the long-term objectives. The development objectives are the strategic marketing objectives, saying where the company is to go, how it is to be seen.

Examples of such objectives would include:

- establish a dominant position in the health-care market;
- initiate projects in Asia and the Middle East;
- increase fee income by 15 per cent per annum.

Development objectives extend over three years. Over a longer period it is difficult to forecast market forces realistically.

Developing the marketing action plan

Strategies are evaluated, measurable tactical objectives are set and tactical marketing plans extending up to one year are developed. These are set within the context of the resources available, and the segmented client needs identified in the analysis stage. An allocation of tasks is made for each variable of the marketing mix – product, price, place, promotion and service. Budgets are allocated.

Performance control

What happens when the marketing plan is implemented? Are the set goals being reached? Are target budgets adequate? Are the marketing constraints as predicted? Successful marketing is a measure of management's flexibility to monitor performance and to adapt to change.

THE INFORMATION NEEDED

Question **What information is needed by management in the analysis stage of a business development programme?**

There are five analysis steps. They seek to analyse resources, and the individual components of the marketplace. The stages are illustrated in Figure 3.2.

Analysis of external environment

The external environment is broken down into a number of component forces and factors:

- client companies, individuals and organizations;
- competitors – existing and potential;
- support organizations – collaborating professional firms, financial institutions, academic institutions;
- the public environment – media, professional organizations, consumer organizations, general public;
- socio-economic forces – the political, economic, technological and social external forces which are beyond the control of the professional firm.

It is productive to conduct the analysis against a grid of opportunities, threats and future potential. A grid is illustrated in Figure 3.3.

Management of threat is important because this activity enables the organization to stay alive. Legislation permitting outsiders to provide financial services to the public – previously the exclusive domain of the banking system – is an example.

Management of opportunity is the jumping-off point for exciting growth. An example would be the relaxation of the advertising constraints imposed by the code of practice of the Institute of Chartered Accountants.

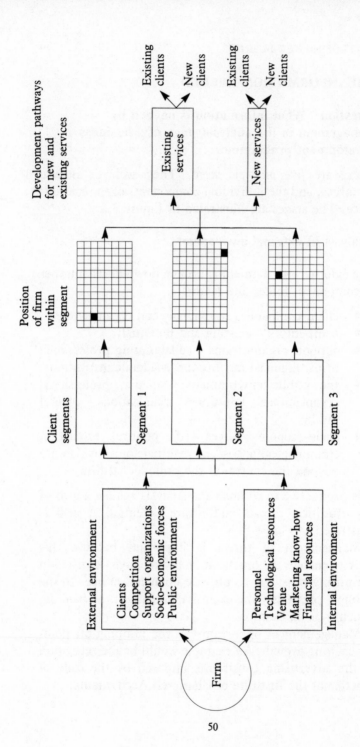

Figure 3.2 Analysis for business development

	Client companies	Competitors	Support organizations	Public environment	Socio-economic forces
Opportunities					
Threats					
Future potential					

Figure 3.3 Opportunities/threat/future potential analysis of the external environment

The future potential derives from the perception of current and historical trends – for example the withdrawal of exchange control regulations in respect of international financial transactions.

Analysis of trade figures and economic performance prior to the legislative change allows a projection of likely change to be made.

Analysis of the internal environment

The internal environment is analysed by means of an internal audit. The objective is to identify what the firm has done, is doing and has the capability to undertake. A useful audit evaluates factors on a scale of one (weak) to five (strong). Figure 3.4 illustrates an internal audit grid. The factors are:

- personnel – professional, management and support;
- technological resources – equipment, academic and published;
- venue – location, number of sites, and appointment and furbishment of offices and professional workplace;
- marketing know-how – current performance at all levels of the company;
- financial resources – actual and potentially available.

Analysis of the contingent marketplace into client segments

Stage 3 analysis is a refinement of the data identified in the preliminary steps of the analysis. The different environments of the professional firm, seen in the context of the resources and skills of that firm, are further

	Weak				Strong
	1	2	3	4	5
Personnel Professional					
Management					
Support					
Technological resources Equipment					
Academic					
Published					
Venue Location					
Number of sites					
Appointment and furbishment of offices and professional workplace					
Marketing know-how Current performance					
Financial resources Actual					
Potential					

Figure 3.4   Analysis of the internal environment

divided into separate segments. Each segment has buyers
sharing identical needs.

There are various bases for segmentation.

- Geographical – clients are identified by the coun-
  ties or towns within which they are based.
- Demographic – age groupings, sex, marital status,
  income, race and education are bases for
  classification.
- Behavioural – groupings are made on the basis of
  performance, usage, habit patterns and degrees of
  loyalty.
- Benefits received – for example, those clients of a
  management training centre who buy consultancy
  as opposed to management training or training
  manuals.

The value to the firm of segmenting the client base is the
opportunity provided for precise marketing planning.
Whether the marketing programme concerns itself with
a single segment or a number of segments is a matter of
judgement. As the basis of segmentation is arbitrary, the
parameters defining each segment reflect the capacity
and skills of the particular firm.

For example, the local chiropodist operating from
home, who does not own a motor car, will target clients
from those living or working nearby.

Analysis of position within segments

The position of a firm within a market segment is, in
effect, the identity of the firm. It is a measure of its skills
and past performance. 'Position' is how a firm is seen
by others so it can be manipulated through marketing
tactics. Figure 3.5 illustrates the position of four architectural practices concerned with private sector dwell-
ings. The parameters of the way in which the firm wants

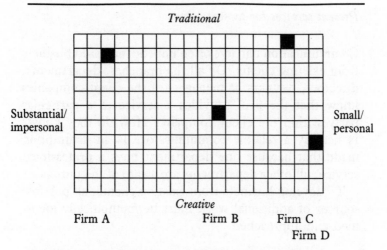

Figure 3.5   Positioning of four architectural firms
            concerned with private sector dwellings

to be judged are arbitrarily set. In Figure 3.5 they are
sets of polar opposites:

- traditional – creative
- substantial/impersonal – small/personal

All staff and personnel should be aware of the position
in the market in which partners of the firm see themselves and towards which they work.

Analysis of pathways of development for existing and new services

There are four pathways for a practice to grow:

- present services for present clients;
- new services for present clients;
- present services for new clients;
- new services for new clients.

Present services for present clients

Communication barriers often impede increased business from existing clients. Do all the branches, departments, directors, partners or managers of the client companies know that the firm provides a service to a particular party within the client company? How do they know? Is hearsay a reliable communicator? Is an assumption made that because one department buys a professional service, all other departments are aware of the purchase?

To develop business from existing clients, all possible sources of additional work must be methodically identified and approached.

New services for present clients

For many professions client development is the greatest source of new business. A recent survey of the accountancy profession revealed that an accountancy practice is often perceived only as the firm carrying out the annual audit; and the audit is a necessary burden imposed by legislation. The survey reported that many firms did not consider seeking their accountant's advice in dealing with any matters outside the strict accounting function. Yet in general terms accountancy offers a wide range of services:

- Auditing
- Special investigations
- VAT, PAYE and national insurance
- Bookkeeping
- Financial advice
- Fraud prevention
- Managing expansion
- New business
- Raising finance

- Government grants
- Corporate taxation
- Personal taxation
- Company secretarial work

The capacity and competence of the individual firm is a function of personnel, experience, resources and motivation, and perhaps an element of luck. Clearly, to build business from existing clients by cross-selling services, the professional firm must be well aware of the wider horizons of professional skills. Without vision, and marketing planning to reach set goals, progress may be slow.

Present services for new clients

Who are the clients from whom business is wanted? In the analysis stage of business development, strategic decisions are not made. The task at this stage is to identify the range of pathways to potential clients. Stage 2 analysis has already set the scene by analysing the firm's marketplace into individual client segments.

Other clients within market segments already served are likely prospects. Analysis of data relating to any existing clients provide useful indicators of the typical client profile. Client needs are known for that segment; and there are guidelines in respect of fee structure.

New services for new clients

This direction is the most difficult for the professional firm. There is no support from an established track record. There is no background of immediately related experience as a yardstick to performance. Notwithstanding this, the momentum of skills within the compass of professional activities may be persuasive enough to initiate business.

BASICS

Question **What are the fundamental questions to be asked in setting development objectives?**

In common with manufacturers of baked beans and supersonic aircraft, the professional firm asks itself the question: 'What business are we in?' In non-marketing terms this is similar to the question: 'What are our long-term objectives?'

There are likely to be many options for progress and growth, but a firm cannot do everything. It is important to decide what major strategies are suitable: perhaps a single strategy, perhaps a number. Resources have already been identified and the needs of clients and potential clients have been defined.

In practical terms setting developmental objectives and strategies sometimes encounters hurdles. Partners within the same firm often have different objectives related to professional, commercial and financial success. But without a common direction, setting tactics for achievement is difficult or impossible.

Alongside the development objectives it is useful to set, explicitly, a statement of the position of the company in its market segments. Position then ranks hand in hand with the objectives as targets of endeavour.

HOW TO GET THERE

Question **What are the essential marketing ingredients of an action plan?**

An action plan sets out the tactics through which development objectives are reached. It is a blueprint for action. The plan is set out in simple, easily read steps, so that it can be implemented smoothly. Plans are of two kinds:

- a marketing launch plan – to initiate a new programme;
- a marketing action plan – to upgrade an earlier marketing initiative.

Within a target period of one year, tactics might be:

- develop and implement an interview programme with clients, suppliers and with staff to identify how they perceive the firm;
- review, upgrade and distribute literature on the firm's activities to all clients and potential clients;
- upgrade the client database, cross-referenced for billable hours, professional skill needs, referral sources and other parameters, and store on computer disc.

The action plan sets short-term objectives, no longer than one year. The management of each variable of the marketing mix – product price, place, promotion and service – is defined. Budgets are allocated. Chapter 5 explains in detail how to prepare an action plan.

THE IMPORTANCE OF CONTROL

Question What does control mean in marketing terms?

Control is the overview of any planned action to see that activities do not diverge from the planned path. In the marketing of services, the requirements of control are compounded. Management has to see that the specific marketing activities are implemented, but other factors also intrude.

Quality control of the services provided   Because services
are often intangible, and are person-intensive, the service
giver must always apply strict quality control. Pressures
are generated by fatigue or distance, or poor environment, or even poor client co-operation. Poor control,
permitting sloppy service, is self-destructive.

Pressures of time   The need for services is often generated spontaneously, for instance toothache or fire hazard.
The obligation of the service supplier to meet an *ad hoc*
service request distorts or erodes planning sequences.
Consequently, the planned marketing activities ancillary
to the core services supplied are diminished or
overlooked.

Contingency planning is a valuable adjunct to the
marketing action plan. It is productive to develop such
a plan at the same time.

SUMMARY

Question   What is the business development path
for the professional firm in a changing marketplace?

Answer   Business development is a multi-stage
process. The stages are:

- analysis;
- setting development objectives;
- developing the marketing action plan;
- performance control.

Question   What information is needed by
management in the analysis stage of a business
development programme?

Answer   There are five discrete steps in the analysis

of client resources and the external marketplace. The
steps are:

- analysis of the external environment;
- analysis of the internal environment;
- analysis of the contingent marketplace into client
  segments;
- analysis of position within segments;
- analysis of pathways of development for existing
  and new services.

**Question What are the fundamental questions to be
asked in setting development objectives?**

Answer The most important question is 'What
business are we in?' Other questions relate to the firm's
long-term objectives balanced against the personal,
professional, financial and commercial objectives of
the partners and directors.

**Question What are the essential marketing
ingredients of an action plan?**

Answer An action plan sets out the short-term
objectives, the budget allocations and the tactics which
enable the firm to meet those objectives. The tactics are
defined with detailed programmes for management of
the marketing mix – product, price, place, promotion
and service.

**Question What does control mean in marketing
terms?**

Answer As action plans are implemented, control is
the flexibility of the firm to adapt and react to changing
circumstances. The problems of control are
compounded both by the requirement for service
quality standards to be maintained and by the

requirement for the service supplier to absorb requests for *ad hoc* delivery of services.

4 Promoting the professional service

Before reading this chapter try to answer the following questions. The material is worked through in the text. Questions and answers appear together at the end of the chapter by way of summary.

QUESTIONS

What does promotion mean in terms of developing new business?

What are the most commonly used promotional tools for the professional firm?

What promotional activities are effective in developing the professional practice?

How is PR best used to generate business for the professional firm?

Chapter 4 synopsis

- Different types of promotion
- Nuts and bolts
- How to generate more business
- Using PR effectively

DIFFERENT TYPES OF PROMOTION

Question   What does promotion mean in terms of developing new business?

Promotion as a specific tool from the marketing mix is a concept new to some. It is designed to put the name, skills and activities of the promoting firm before existing and potential clients. Sometimes there is confusion between promotional activities and public relations activities. Neither is clearly differentiated from advertising, and advertising is far from straightforward due to the guidelines and/or restraints imposed by some professions. Each is in turn defined below.

Advertising

In advertising, a message is conveyed through one or more media. The principal categories of media are newspapers, journals, directories, magazines, radio, television, outdoor billboards and computer-linked viewdata systems. The advertising is paid for by the firm initiating the message. Control of the message therefore lies with the advertiser, subject only to ethical constraints.

Media bookings are secured through advertising

agencies. Traditionally, agencies are paid a commission of 15 per cent from the media owners. More and more the practice is developing for agencies also to charge a service fee to the advertisers for the comprehensive services rendered.

PR

PR covers that range of communication about a firm or practitioner which is outside advertising. Advertising and PR are often complementary. The PR message is published without direct payment but, because no payment is charged by the media owners, the company or partnership to whom the message relates has no direct control over the message.

PR does involve costs. To secure PR, factual messages must be supplied to the media owners. This requires time and expertise. Messages written in the style of the journal, paper or radio programme are more readily accepted when little editorial attention is required. PR agencies, in the nature of their work, offer the skills required to write press releases in the relevant styles. They also have the contacts and resources to secure publication. Fees are charged for this professional service.

The scope of PR is wide. It is not restricted only to routine press releases on the appointments of new partners or the opening of new offices. It may involve providing speakers from within the firm to address the local chamber of commerce, or a charity fête; or providing the in-house expert to review publications and articles on specialist subjects. Arranging an open day for members of the public and invited guests to see the activities of the firm would be good PR. So too would mounting seminars with in-house and guest speakers.

Promotion

Promotional material comprises all printed matter which is not specifically advertising or PR copy. Brochures, letterheads, visiting cards, leaflets and printed envelopes are all forms of promotional material. Promotional activities for the professional firm are described as those activities designed to promote the image and progress of the firm. Promotional objectives are to:

- build awareness amongst potential users;
- differentiate service from that of competitors;
- communicate the benefits of using the company services;
- build a favourable image;
- persuade customers to use the company's services;
- eliminate preconceived misconceptions – if any exist;
- advise existing and potential clients of new resources.

NUTS AND BOLTS

Question **What are the most commonly used promotional tools for the professional firm?**

In the current marketplace, client tastes are frequently sophisticated. The marketing tools to communicate with those clients must therefore match in the level of sophistication and message. The promotional tools described below are used by most companies.

Brochures

As a rough rule of thumb, the costs of production divide into 25 per cent for design, 25 per cent for text copy and 50 per cent for printing. Economizing by undertaking design or copywriting in house is sometimes counter-productive. Criticism of syntax or literary style is not always easy to accept, and personal issues intrude. This is especially so when the author or artist has other professional skills of unquestionably high calibre.

The company brochure is an extremely important document. It speaks on behalf of the firm and it has a specific role to play – but it does not exist in isolation. The brochure must integrate with letterheads, packaging and the overall styling of the company, including the appointment and decor of the company premises.

There is a low-cost method of integrating the design image of a company, with special reference to the production of a brochure and literature. It is to give the problem task to a school of art as a project for a degree course or for post-graduate students. Charges are likely to be on a materials cost basis with perhaps a service fee, but total costs would be substantially lower than those in the marketplace.

However the brochure, letterheads and logo are produced, the image of the company is first promoted by the visual impact. Before even the first words of the copy are read an image message is given. So the company must know what it wants to say. Does it want to emulate others in the profession? Is it important that the company is seen to be different, creative, traditional, trustworthy, trailblazing? The reaction of a representative section of the public to the mock-ups of the brochure should be tested.

In respect of the brochure message there is just one basic ground rule: Describe the *benefits* available to clients.

Potted histories of the partners with their qualifications are useful, especially when the company is small. So are other features that tell about the company structure, venue and resources. But readers of the brochure want to know first and foremost what can be done to satisfy their needs. It is only of secondary, albeit contingent, importance to describe exactly who provides the professional skills and how, when and where.

Newsletters

Newsletters are an important tool, provided that they carry out their intended function. In-house newsletters are an effective medium for promulgating news of in-house happenings: news of promotions, club outings and even classified advertisments all have a place within the company. But they do not necessarily stimulate interest for clients and potential clients placed on the circulation list.

Newsletters must be produced with professional skill. Editorial skills and graphic design can be bought in if they are not present. Company-related news – such as new projects, or past and recent successes – is effective in stimulating interest. So are the achievements and honours of company personnel.

With a small advertising appropriation, the alternative option of circulating a regular newsletter to a selected list of organizations and clients is worth considering.

Video films

With video the opportunities for presenting the successes and skills of the company are considerable. Aside from professional restraints, the major constraining factor is cost. There is a wide spectrum of quality, ranging from DIY 'home movies' standard to broadcast quality. This is reflected in the cost. But the 'home movies' standard is unlikely to make a significant contribution to promotional achievement.

One effective method of keeping costs down is to take a series of still photographs. These are skilfully converted into a video presentation with captions and a linked commentary.

Synchronized tape/slide presentations

This medium is similar in approach to the linked stills photographs of video production. Again there is a spectrum of quality, in terms of the hardware employed. Generally, costs of tape/slide production are less than for video films.

Two significant benefits of the tape/slide presentation are the opportunities afforded to update the material used with minimal effort and to tailor the material specifically to client needs.

Press releases

Press releases give factual information relating to a firm's activities. They can be one-sentence releases, such as 'Planning permission was today secured by Urban Developments Ltd for the construction of a multi-storey car park on the Hillside Farm Estate', or the information is given in a multi-column article complete with photographs, captions and descriptive copy.

A press release may take the form of a background story providing the historical link to the present day, or it is presented with a description and full technical story.

Yet another form of press release is the digest of a speech or report. The more closely the 'style' of the release matches the style of the journal or paper, the greater the likelihood of publication. New releases are also used by the television stations and by the BBC and local radio stations.

Press and news releases should state:

- the subject of the story;
- the name and address of the organization;
- description, specification and details of the project/activity giving the salient features that make it of interest;
- the benefits to the community, and to the readers, listeners or viewers;
- contacts for further information.

Exhibitions

Exhibitions designed to promote professional services differ little from those promoting commercial products. Of necessity there are no tangible products to see, but there may be records, photographs, models, audio-tape and video-tape recordings of performances and achievements. There may also be testimonials.

Of equal importance is the opportunity for visitors to the exhibition to discuss what they see, either on a stand at the exhibition itself or subsequently with the firm concerned.

Exhibitions contribute to progress in other ways. There is the opportunity for feedback on happenings and events within the profession. There is the opportunity for the release of information on innovative skills or processes or research achievements. Furthermore, principal/agent relationships can be struck. Persons and companies able to deliver services remote from the service source are able to make contacts and perhaps negotiate agreements.

To be effective in their work, exhibition organizers must generate interest from target audience segments related to the exhibition theme. There is certain to be a throughput of visitors to the exhibition which is complementary to the invited guests of individual exhibitors.

Selection of office site

The siting of the professional office is an important promotional tool – whether it is a clinic, a surgery or a straightforward workplace. The attitude of the client is influenced by the ease of access, of parking, and the halo effect of the geographical location itself.

Is the office convenient for frequently used facilities, and are services such as banks, finance houses and printing or design offices situated locally? Is the office near to suppliers of competitive services? It is important to the practitioner to have restaurants or clubs nearby for entertainment. The costs of the site, in terms of mortgages, leases, security and parking, are also significant.

HOW TO GENERATE MORE BUSINESS

Question **What promotional activities are effective in developing the professional practice?**

Some activities are very successful indeed in increasing business for the professional person; others are used less frequently. But promotion as a marketing tool is a planned activity. The likely success of a promotional initiative must be something for which a projection can be made. In this way the return on investment from the marketing appropriation can be predicted with some degree of accuracy.

Client contact

Except in those professions where the concept is proscribed, client contact means personal selling. Client personnel are methodically targeted; for example, the purchasing manager, the local authority treasurer or the process equipment design office manager is singled out for contact and discussion. When permitted, a direct approach by letter or phone call asks for a meeting. Alternatively, effort is directed to ensure that a 'chance' meeting occurs. At such a meeting, the marketing effort is continued to generate in the targeted contact the interest to ask about the professional activities, resources and experience of the person 'selling'.

Success in selling results from identifying and satisfying client needs. Services (and products) carry benefits. The same service offers different benefits to different users. For example, the contact lens optician sells beauty to the young girl who shuns glasses, and improved vision to the athlete involved in contact sports. So the early stages of client contact are structured in identifying client needs as accurately as possible. How the benefits from the services available can meet those needs are then described and at what cost and effort on the part of the client.

Personal selling skills are learned. Many in the professions are insulated from the street wisdom of commercial life. Selling is not a natural component of everyday intercourse. So the selling steps – qualifying needs, matching needs with benefits, overcoming objections and closing for a sale – can be learned and practised. Selling for the professional becomes a discipline, hand in hand with the discipline of marketing activities and the discipline of the profession itself.

Sponsorship

Sponsorship is an excellent medium for placing the name of a company before the public. The sponsor undertakes financial responsibility for sporting, cultural, theatrical and charitable events. Academic sponsorship for research and training is also known. The sponsorship is undertaken on a national, regional or local basis.

The return to the sponsor consists of enhanced publicity and public exposure of the firm's name to a cross-section of the population. Sponsorship of the arts – whether music, painting, ballet, sculpture, photography or literature – (and there is much else) – is different from sponsorship of sport. There is a perceived element of social responsibility and the dignified image with which professional firms are wont to be associated. Sponsorship of the arts can take the form of exhibitions, awards, grants, master classes or competitions.

There are some tax advantages in respect of sponsorship. Payments made under deed of covenant to organizations that are registered charities are eligible for relief from income tax or corporation tax. The matter is clarified in a booklet, *Industrial Sponsorship and Joint Promotions*, published by the Directory of Social Change, 9 Mansfield Place, London NW3.

Writing for publication

The objective of writing is to have the name of the writer and his firm in the public eye. One option is writing letters on topical matters to the editor of prestigious newspapers, Sunday papers, magazines and journals. Another option is an article on an aspect of professional practice. When writing skills have been identified within a firm, the problem to overcome is usually practical rather than literary: time to be spent on writing is difficult to find. But promoting the company through writing is but one marketing tool. Promotional tasks should be allocated to all concerned with the development of the company.

Community involvement

A starting point is to list all possible areas of involvement – juvenile delinquent rehabilitation, care of the aged, youth groups, sport, education, medical ethics and environmental care. There are many areas that welcome application and energy, albeit on the basis of only one or two hours a week or month. The first question to answer is whether there is genuine interest in making a contribution.

A spin-off in the form of business contact is likely to follow from community involvement, but it is important that interest is not superficial. Lack of genuine interest is difficult to disguise.

Membership of a professional body

The immediate return from membership of a professional body is self-development. An awareness is maintained of trends and changes in professional attitudes and thought. Contacts are developed and reinforced. But by being active within the professional body there is also an opportunity to establish a personal reputation; this itself is a form of promotion.

Referrals from existing clients

In some professions – accountancy is one, insurance another – referrals are the biggest source of new business. Some referrals occur spontaneously: this is a bonus, no marketing effort has been spent. But it is essential that the client giving the recommendation is contacted and thanked. Clearly the client was satisfied with the service received, to the extent that he or she described it to others.

The professional company must make it a practice to identify the source of all new clients. In this way the referring sources within the client base are identified and mapped. This highlights the clients from which no referrals are provided: are they dissatisfied with the service or services provided? If not, what can be done to nudge the clients into making recommendations?

One method is to ask the inactive client if his name may be given to others as a referee. Such a question is prefaced by an enquiry to ascertain that the client is satisfied with the service provided. Another method is to ask the client directly if he or she would recommend the firm to others. Again, the first priority is to be sure that the level of service received is totally satisfactory.

Developing the practice through referral is an ongoing process; it is a planned activity. Responsibility for ensuring that referrals occur should be allocated to a partner as a marketing task.

USING PR EFFECTIVELY

Question **How is PR best used to generate business for the professional firm?**

Public relations is a communication tool, itself a component activity of the marketing function. The principal task of public relations is to develop and maintain the image of a firm. It does this by influencing attitudes. A difference between marketing and PR is that the former tries to manipulate behaviour in a specific way, for example by the adoption or change of a buying decision pattern. PR is concerned with arousing interest. The public relations process in Figure 4.1 shows the pathway to generating good PR.

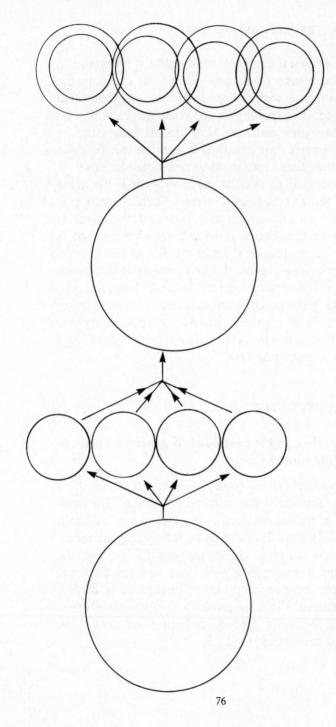

Stage 1: Identify
images of the different
publics

Stage 2: Carry
out image
audit

Stage 3: Establish
image objectives

Stage 4: Develop
PR strategies

Figure 4.1 The PR process

Stage 1

The first step in making use of PR is to identify the different public images of the firm. They are illustrated in detail in Figure 4.2.

- Media
- Professional association
- Competitors
- Potential clients
- Clients
- Financial institutions
- Government agencies
- Consumer movements
- Firm's employees
- Community groups

Stage 2

An image audit for each of these publics is carried out to identify the nature of each image. Whilst the images are unlikely to be identified much overlap is usual. An audit format is set out below. This is likely to vary as a function of the profession.

Format for an image audit

Thank you for agreeing to this meeting. We are researching to identify the present image of the company. May I please have your answers to a few questions? It would be helpful if the answers are all rated from bad to good on a scale of one to five: one is very bad; five is very good

- What is the image of our profession?
- What is the quality of the services provided by our company?

Figure 4.2   The different public images of the professional firm

- How competent technically are those services?
- What is the quality of competitors' services?
- How effectively does the company demonstrate that it cares for your particular needs?
- How effectively does the geographical position of the company relate to your needs?
- How effectively does the company communicate with you?
- How competitive are the company's fees?
- How does the image of the company relate to the image of the profession as a whole?
- How do you perceive the professional resources of the company?

- How do you perceive the track record of the company?
- What is the quality of management of the company?
- What do you consider is the financial strength of the company?
- How effectively is client contact administered?
- How do you rate the company's efforts to publicize itself?
- How creative is the company in problem-solving?
- What do you consider to be the company's prospects for growth: – in the short term? – in the medium term?
- How do you view the quality of marketing?
- How effective are back-up services?

Thank you for those answers. One last question please: What do you consider are the company's strengths and weaknesses?

Stage 3

PR image objectives are set reflecting how the practice is to be seen. The objectives should relate comprehensively to the desired images of skills, experience, position, achievement, understanding of client needs, resources, personnel and all the important factors which influence the placing of business.

Stage 4

PR strategies are developed for each of the major publics. It is important that the strategies are cost-effective in meeting the set objectives. For example, an elaborate, multi-coloured brochure with many pages may be particularly dignified and attractive – but it may be only marginally more effective than a simpler, much less expensive brochure.

Because the different publics are likely to see the firm in different ways, strategies will differ. In some cases literature and correspondence are adequate; in others a face-to-face presentation or mounting a seminar are more suitable.

The day-to-day behaviour of all in the firm contributes to PR. It is important that each person is aware of the contribution that he or she makes, in every aspect of the daily workload.

SUMMARY

Question   **What does promotion mean in terms of developing new business?**

Answer   Promotion is a marketing concept. It is a specific tool from the marketing mix designed to put the name and activities of the promoting body before existing and potential clients.

Question   **What are the most commonly used promotional tools for the professional firm?**

Answer   Important promotional tools are brochures, newsletters, video films, synchronized tape/slide presentations, press releases and the selection of the office site.

Question   **What promotional activities are effective in developing the professional practice?**

Answer   There are a number of practical promotional activities: client contact, sponsorship, writing for publication, community involvement, membership of a professional body, exhibitions, obtaining referrals and PR.

Question How is PR best used to generate business for the professional firm?

Answer PR develops and maintains the image of a firm as seen by the different publics with which the firm interacts. PR strategies are developed to meet set image objectives.

5 The marketing plan

Before reading this chapter try to answer the following questions. The material is worked through in the text. Questions and answers appear together at the end of the chapter by way of summary.

QUESTIONS

What is the function of the marketing plan?

What format is helpful in preparing a marketing plan?

What are the main features of a marketing plan?

What detailed areas of marketing performance demand regular effort to contribute to practice progress?

What marketing ingredients of a client development

programme should be incorporated in the marketing plan?

What are the main types of information that need to be collected in a marketing plan?

Chapter 5 synopsis

- Why have a plan?
- The format to use
- Steps for action
- Aspects of good marketing
- Marketing for client development
- Useful information

WHY HAVE A PLAN?

Question   What is the function of the marketing plan?

Marketing is a discipline. Marketing action is most effective when the relevant activities are planned and co-ordinated. The marketing plan is a blueprint to structure responsibilities and actions. It identifies the objectives to be achieved, the resources to be used, the place and the time scale of the operation.

There are two types of marketing plan.

The marketing launch plan   This plan is prepared for the development of a new market or new discipline or new programme of expansion.

The marketing action plan   This plan describes the forth-coming planning stage of an existing practice operation.

Although there is no hard and fast rule, a marketing

plan is unlikely to be a totally effective instrument for a period longer than twelve months. External forces change; it is difficult to predict their nature and course with accuracy for much longer than this period. So for the period from the start day of a new operation to day 365 there can be one marketing plan, or a number of updated plans. The more variables that have to be researched, the more difficult it is to set realistic objectives. For example, a marketing launch plan is most realistic when the parameters of external variables such as competition, client needs, disposable income levels, or environmental, social or cultural constraints have already been identified through research. The planner's judgement of resources necessary to overcome market hurdles is then linked to experience and available data, rather than conjecture.

THE FORMAT TO USE

Question   **What format is helpful in preparing a marketing plan?**

The marketing plan is a document describing a course or courses of action. It relates to activities within criteria set or defined by the planner. The starting point is the aims of the company.

Figure 5.1 illustrates a format helpful in the preparation of a marketing plan. The plan is a progression of individual steps, each step being a compilation of research data, a planning support activity or a marketing activity task.

Aims of the company   The aims are what the company hopes to achieve in the medium and long term.

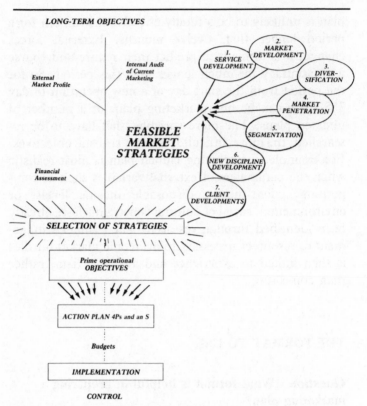

LONG-TERM OBJECTIVES

FEASIBLE MARKET STRATEGIES

1. SERVICE DEVELOPMENT
2. MARKET DEVELOPMENT
3. DIVER-SIFICATION
4. MARKET PENETRATION
5. SEGMENTATION
6. NEW DISCIPLINE DEVELOPMENT
7. CLIENT DEVELOPMENTS

External Market Profile

Internal Audit of Current Marketing

Financial Assessment

SELECTION OF STRATEGIES

Prime operational OBJECTIVES

ACTION PLAN 4Ps and an S

Budgets

IMPLEMENTATION

CONTROL

Figure 5.1   Preparing the marketing plan

External market profile   Who are the clients and potential clients? Who are the competitors, and the support organizations?

What is known about the environment in which the company practises? What economic or professional forces constrain or reinforce progress? The answers to the questions provide the data on the external market.

Internal audit of current marketing performance   It is necessary to know what marketing skills and capabilities are immediately available. What marketing skills are available in-house? What skills have to be bought in, and at what cost?

Feasible market strategies   The options are:

- Service development
- Market development
- Diversification
- Market penetration
- Segmentation
- New discipline development
- Client development

Financial assessment   What are the financial resources available? What potential resources can be tapped?

Selection of strategies   One or more of the strategies is selected in the light of the external forces to be met, and the professional, personnel and financial resources available.

Prime operational objectives   Objectives are set which are precise and quantifiable.

Action plan – marketing mix tactics for product, price, place, promotion and service   The activities for each of the marketing mix factors are detailed and allocated in turn. The task of each person responsible for marketing action is set out. There is the additional responsibility for motivating everyone in the firm to carry out non-specific marketing action.

Budgets   Budgets are set for each of the four Ps and an S, allowing a contingency sum to deal with the unplanned hurdles that often arise.

Implementation and control   The plan is set in action as

prescribed. Achievements are monitored carefully. Successful plans have a built-in flexibility to accommodate the unexpected happening.

STEPS FOR ACTION

Question **What are the main features of a marketing plan?**

The main features of the marketing plan are the same, whether the firm is a sole practitioner or very large. The structure follows the format shown in the last section. Such differences as do exist lie in the size and complexity of the plan. The length of the marketing plan is not significant. What is important is that the content provides a basis from which to work.

The starting point is to state the corporate aims of the firm. Often they are just taken for granted. The aims answer the marketing questions: 'What business are we in?' and 'Where do we want to go?'

It is important to identify the person in the firm whose task is to control and follow through the implementation of the plan. In a small firm, or in the case of a sole practitioner, the plan leader undertakes all responsibility. In the larger firm this can be a marketing co-ordinator. He or she can be supported by a marketing committee drawn from different departments or divisions of the firm. Each is responsible for allocated activities within the plan. Figure 5.2 is the start document. It sets the scene.

Succeeding pages of the marketing plan set out the programme of activities. Figure 5.3 deals with the external environment, Figure 5.4 with internal resources. The success of the implemented marketing plan derives from the action taken. A plan by itself achieves nothing, no matter how grandiose. There has to be overall control and motivation, and individual commitment and participation. Successful marketing means research, planning, setting targets, action and regular review meetings.

There are additional activities that contribute to achievement of the marketing objectives. Figure 5.5 sets out the marketing awareness programme.

Figure 5.6 deals with the activities contributing to effective marketing communication. Within the limited period of a marketing plan some of the activities may be one-off, or even not undertaken at all if they were dealt with in the recent past. An example is the integration of brochure, literature and letterhead in a single, compelling design concept.

ASPECTS OF GOOD MARKETING

Question **What detailed areas of marketing performance demand regular effort to contribute to practice progress?**

Some marketing activities are small and insignificant when viewed out of context. They are everyday personal actions. Answering the telephone to callers is one example, personal salutations are another. So is making sure that messages left are delivered to the intended person. Part of any marketing plan must be a planned regular commitment to ensure that every action which might otherwise prejudice client response is performed to a high standard. Wherever possible a standardized procedure should be introduced for office personnel. In this way stress and the avoidance of difficult decision-making are removed from newly appointed and junior staff faced with client contact. Evaluation of performance

TITLE: _____

PLAN LEADER: _____ DATE: _____

  COMMITTEE: _____

  MEMBERS: _____

CORPORATE
AIMS: _____

STRATEGIC   1. _____
OBJECTIVES: _____
                         2. _____
                         _____
                         3. _____
                         _____

TERRITORY: _____

PERIOD OF PLAN: From: _____
                To: _____

PERSONNEL   1. _____
INVOLVED: 2. _____
                         3. _____
                         4. _____
                         5. _____

BUDGET
ALLOCATION: _____

Contingency budget _____
allocation

RESOURCES   (a) _____
ALLOCATION: (b) _____
                         (c) _____
                         (d) _____

Figure 5.2   The marketing plan: document 1: The plan

ACTION TACTICS: 1. _____
Target date: _____
                 2. _____
Target date: _____
                 3. _____
Target date: _____

1. EXTERNAL ENVIRONMENT

Controlled by: _____
Date: _____

Client segment A

	1	2	3	4	5	6	7

Positional statement: The firm is seen as:

Dominant/weak

Creative/traditional

Financially strong/weak

Professionally competent/incompetent

Major clients (fee billings over £X000)   _____
                                               _____

Growth potential clients   _____
                                               _____

Referral sources   _____

Media support – actual   _____

              – potential   _____

Collaborating professionals   _____
                                               _____

Major competition   _____
                                               _____

Figure 5.2 **(concluded)**

Client segment B

	1	2	3	4	5	6	7
Positional statement: The firm is seen as:							
Dominant/weak							
Creative/traditional							

Financially strong/weak

Professionally competent/incompetent

Major clients (fee billings over £X000)   _____

Growth potential clients   _____

Referral sources   _____

Media support – actual   _____

         – potential   _____

Collaborating professionals   _____

Major competition   _____

**Figure 5.3   The marketing plan: document 2: Strategic
analysis of the external environment**

2. INTERNAL RESOURCES   Controlled by: _____
                                     Date: _____

Professional skills   _____
                                     _____
                                     _____
                                     _____

Representation on professional bodies _____
                                     _____

Representation on civil, political cultural, _____
environmental bodies   _____

Marketing communication channels   _____
                                     _____

Public relations programmes   _____
                                     _____

Client development programmes   _____
                                     _____

Marketing know-how   _____

Marketing information systems:

    Control   _____

    Distribution   _____

Marketing performance review programme _____

Marketing training resources:

    In-house   _____

    External   _____

**Figure 5.4   The marketing plan: document 3: Strategic
            analysis of the internal environment**

Controlled by: _____
Date: _____

Existing contact dates

    Client A _____
    Client B _____
    Client C _____

Prospective client contact dates

    Client D _____
    Client E _____
    Client F _____

Public speaking activities

Organization G _____ Speaker _____ Venue _____ Date _____

           H _____   _____   _____   _____

           I _____   _____   _____   _____

Planned social participations

Event   J _____ Venue _____ Date _____

           K _____   _____   _____

           L _____   _____   _____

Community activities

Committee   M _____ Venue _____ Date _____

           N _____   _____   _____

           O _____   _____   _____

Seminar activities

    In-house   _____   Date: _____
                                                             _____

    External   _____   Date: _____
                                                             _____

Figure 5.5   The marketing plan: document 4: Awareness programme

Design and produce brochure   Target date:_____

Distribute brochure   Target date:_____

Integrate the design and production of
firm's logo literature and letterheads
with brochure   Target date:_____

Undertake programme of press
releases   Target date:_____

Circulate skills index in-house and to
selected clients   Target date:_____

Produce and distribute newsletter   Person responsible: _____

Undertake prospecting direct mail
campaign   Person responsible: _____

Implement advertising campaign   Target date:_____

**Figure 5.6   The marketing plan: document 5:
Communication activities**

is achieved through third party contacts made on a
regular basis at different times of the day. Scoring is
marked on a five-point scale:

- Very poor: 1
- Poor: 2
- Indifferent: 3
- Efficient: 4
- Very efficient: 5

Figure 5.7, Client service level improvement
programme, incorporates a check on pertinent service
activities.

Compiled by: _____
Date: _____

Telephone answering skills   Monitoring dates: _____

Face-to-face contact of office
personnel with clients/public   Monitoring dates: _____

Client enquiry response lead   Average time for ten random
time   selected enquiries: _____

Tidiness/comfort of client
waiting rooms (bad/average/
good)   Monitoring dates: _____

Age of waiting-room reading   Average age for ten random
material   selected inspections: _____

Efficiency of reception staff
(bad/average/good)   Monitoring dates: _____

**Figure 5.7   The marketing plan: document 6: Client
service level improvement programme**

MARKETING FOR CLIENT DEVELOPMENT

Question   **What marketing ingredients of a client
development programme should be incorporated in
the marketing plan?**

Client development does not happen by itself: constant
planned pressure and effort are necessary. Clients must
hold a favourable image of the service supplier. The
image has to be known, so that appropriate action is
taken if it is not favourable. What the client thinks is
ascertained by interview – usually at partner level.

Publicity relating to available resources, service

capacity and service levels should discreetly bombard decision-makers in the client company. In addition, the client's professional support service supplies – bankers, lawyers, accountants, advertising agents and so on – have to be kept informed of the skills and initiatives available.

Figure 5.8 covers the actions important in generating increased business from existing clients.

USEFUL INFORMATION

Question   **What are the main types of information that need to be collected in a marketing plan?**

Before many marketing plans are developed preliminary research seeks to establish a wide base of data. But there is an ongoing need for pertinent data. Certain strata of information should be compiled and stored for future application. This onerous task is greatly facilitated by computer application.

Figure 5.9 provides a discipline for information collection and storage in parallel with the other marketing plan activities.

SUMMARY

Question   **What is the function of the marketing plan?**

Answer   The marketing plan is a blueprint for action designed to attract client interest, instructions and response.

Question   **What format is helpful in preparing a marketing plan?**

Controller: _____
Date: _____

Identify target major clients

A _____

B _____

C _____

Identify target clients of significant potential

D _____

E _____

Identify clients as referral sources

F _____

G _____

Identify client professional support firms

H _____

I _____

Conduct research interviews with above target firms

Dates: _____ _____ _____ _____

Direct promotional campaign to target bodies

Dates: _____ _____ _____ _____

Mount complementary services selling campaign to target firms

Dates: _____ _____ _____ _____

**Figure 5.8   The marketing plan: document 7: Client
development programme**

Implement planned programme of social civic contact with clients

Dates: _____ _____ _____ _____

Expand network contacts of firm personnel with client staff

Client J _____ K _____ L _____ M _____

Monitor appointments of decision-making new personnel in client firms

Client N_____ O _____ P _____ Q _____

Figure 5.8   (concluded)

Answer   The starting point of any plan is the overall aims of the firm. The external and internal environments of the firm are identified and evaluated so that specific marketing objectives can be set. The parameters of the plan are the marketing and professional skills of the company together with the financial resources. Tactical actions are developed so that within set budgets the strategic marketing objectives are reached.

Question   **What are the main features of a marketing plan?**

Answer   The main features of a plan are a series of checklist documents covering the whole activity framework. Persons in authority, territorial areas, budgets, action tactics and resources to be used are specified. In addition, detailed lists are incorporated in respect of internal and external marketing research, individual marketing actions, marketing awareness tasks, client development activities and information gathering.

Controlled by: _____

Date: _____

Attach separate data sheets as appropriate

Client profiles

A _____ B _____ C _____ D _____ E _____

Professional skills index

F _____ G _____ H _____ I _____ J _____

Fees billed

(a) By client segment: K _____ L _____ M _____ N _____

(b) Through referral source: O _____ P _____

(c) By area: Q _____ R _____

(d) Network contacts: S _____ T _____ U _____

Marketplace reports/surveys

V _____ W _____ X _____ Y _____ Z _____

The competition

Professional skills   _____

Technology   _____

Contracts taken   _____

Personnel seen as threats _____

**Figure 5.9   The marketing plan: document 8: Information
                system**

Question **What detailed areas of marketing performance demand regular effort to contribute to practice progress?**

Answer To achieve marketing excellence, attention must be paid to detail. In respect of face-to-face and telephone contact, personnel and management behaviour alike must be of a constant high standard. All levels of interface between the firm and its clients and its public have to be of the same high standard. This applies both to behavioural and environmental aspects.

Question **What marketing ingredients of a client development programme should be incorporated in the marketing plan?**

Answer The ingredients of a marketing plan for client development are:

- up-to-date awareness of the firm's public images;
- ongoing planned publicity about professional resources to client decision-makers and service support organizations;
- a selling campaign for complementary services.

Question **What are the main types of information that need to be collected in a marketing plan?**

Answer All information having application to practice development is important. Examples are client profiles, an index of professional skills available from the firm, analyses of fee income identified from different source areas, network contacts, marketplace reports and surveys. In addition data, on competitive skills, performance, successes and personnel are of practical use.

PART II
The Skills of Marketing

6 Making a presentation

Before reading this chapter try to answer the following questions. The material is worked through in the text. Questions and answers appear together at the end of the chapter by way of summary.

QUESTIONS

What questions should be asked when a presentation is to be made?

What are the practical aspects of preparing to make a presentation?

What kinds of visual aids contribute to a presentation?

What are the 'golden rules' for using visual aids?

What is the best format for an effective presentation?

What self-help action leads to improved performance?

Chapter 6 synopsis

- Preparing for the presentation
- Practical steps
- The importance of visual aids
- A set of golden rules
- Planning for the talking
- Improvement starts at home

PREPARING FOR THE PRESENTATION

Question **What question should be asked when a presentation is to be made?**

In an effective presentation, the interest of the audience is captured from the outset – and it is held throughout. But good speaking does not happen by itself: the presentation is planned precisely. The answers to the following questions provide the necessary structure: Why? Who? What? How? Where? and When? Figure 6.1 shows this in diagrammatic form.

Why is this presentation being made?

A presentation is made for many reasons. The speaker may want to sell to the audience, or he may want the listeners to embrace a course of action proposed in the presentation. The presentation may be designed to allay fears and apprehensions known to be present. It is important that the objectives of the presentation are clearly stated.

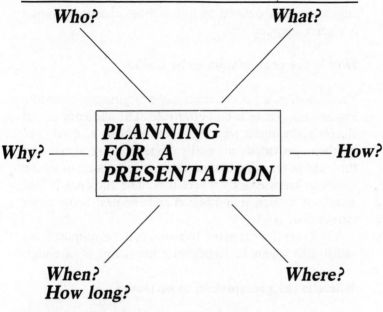

Figure 6.1   Planning for a presentation

Who is listening?

It is important to identify the people in the audience. What are their names, or at least the names of those likely to influence decision-making or press coverage? What is their status? Are there known facts about the audience in respect of achievements, or social/political/professional commitments? Is there an existing relationship between the presenter and some of the audience?

What is to be said in the presentation?

The subject matter relates to the set objectives of the presentation – they must therefore be met. Apprehensions and anxieties of the audience are allayed. The audi-

ence's reaction desired to follow from the presentation
is clearly mapped out.

How is the presentation to be made?

Traditionally, a presentation has a beginning, a middle
and an end. There is no better rule. The audience is told
clearly at the outset what it is about to hear. The material
is then provided in easily digestible sections and
throughout the presentation there are signposts to let the
audience know exactly where it is. The audience is told
when one section is completed and the next about to be
introduced.

A full text is written out initially, and the support from
visual aids planned. Rehearsing the script is essential.

Where is the presentation to be made?

The speaker and all likely to attend a presentation must
know exactly where the presentation is to be given.
Appropriate arrangements, such as the booking of a
room or hall, lecture theatre or hotel, must be dealt with.
Contingent arrangements in respect of notifying all who
should attend are also made.

At the venue, all audio visual equipment is checked.
The seating is laid out so that the audience can hear
clearly. Suitable instructions are given so that interruptions are prevented. Arrangements are also necessary
to deal with incoming phone calls for members of the
audience.

When is it time to start and stop?

Timing needs careful planning. Presentations usually
form part of a schedule, so the start and finish times are
important. Time may be needed for questions to be

asked and answered. Time is often required to allow for registration and for administration.

PRACTICAL STEPS

Question **What are the practical aspects of preparing to make a presentation?**

The first step is to identify the needs of the audience. What are their names and positions? What are their specific responsibilities or interests? Do they control important budgets? What are the constraints imposed by the profession or the presenter's own company? Such information as is appropriate is obtained. Next, facts to support the objectives of the presentation are necessary, but they should relate also to the needs of the target audience.

The material of the presentation is best assembled initially in note form prior to writing it out in full. It is best structured with a strong opening and a strong finish. A good opening is essential to grasp and hold the audience's attention. A short, pithy statement followed by a pause is effective. Quotations and aphorisms are usually successful, and are also effective at the end. Ideally, a presentation finishes on a climax which leaves the audience thinking and talking about what has been said.

Within the presentation important and critical points are given special prominence. This is achieved through voice modulation, by emphasis and by repetition.

When the material has been fully assembled the presentation should be written out in full, word by word. In this way it can be timed: it also allows the structure and the message to be evaluated. The length of presentation has often to be tailored to fit the available time. It is helpful to time each section of the presentation, so that if time runs out during the actual presentation the speaker is better prepared to adapt and change.

The written presentation is then condensed. A highlight pen is used to point up the opening words of each paragraph and the salient points within that paragraph. The presentation is rehearsed – with rehearsal comes fluency. Soon, words in the different paragraphs can be eliminated. With practice and with repetition the major part of the fully written speech is cut away, without diminishing the message or the delivery.

Postcard-sized cards are ideal to take the notes of a presentation. They are numbered in sequence. It is productive to punch a hole in the top right-hand corner of the cards and thread them together with a legal tag. Each card is then turned over during the presentation when the notes have been used. Note cards loosely held together have been known to be out of order during a presentation: the situation is worse if the cards are dropped.

THE IMPORTANCE OF VISUAL AIDS

Question **What kinds of visual aids contribute to a presentation?**

Visual aids reinforce a presentation. Providing additional emphasis by means other than sound can be most valuable.

Blackboard

Many older-style training rooms have a blackboard.

Advantages It is easy to move about; it is simple to use to list points which arise.

Disadvantages Chalk dust tends to get everywhere; blackboards are not a permanent display; there is a limited writing area; it is difficult to prepare a blackboard and keep it hidden until the appropriate time; after constant use a blackboard begins to look very untidy; writing on a blackboard is quite difficult; when writing the presenter has his or her back to the audience.

Whiteboard

Whiteboards are the modern equivalent of blackboards and are usually found in recently constructed training rooms. Felt-tip crayons are used instead of chalk. The surface is wiped clean with an impregnated or damp cloth.

Advantages The advantages are similar to those of blackboard, plus there is no chalk dust.

Disadvantages Similar to those of blackboards.

Flip charts

Advantages Flip charts are portable; they provide a permanent record; the flip-chart sheets can be pre-prepared and kept covered until required; multi-coloured felt-tip crayons are available for emphasis; the charts can be kept clean and tidy; it is easy to record points arising during a presentation or meeting, without having the presenter's back to the audience whilst writing.

Disadvantages There is limited space; it is necessary to write tidily; there is a tendency to scribble.

Overhead slide projectors

Advantages   The slides can be pre-prepared using multi-coloured letters and designs; the headings and words of a prepared slide enable a presenter to dispense with notes; additional trigger words can be written on the cardboard mounts holding the slide; slides offer a dramatic emphasis to subject areas; overhead slides are simple to use; portable projectors are available; one faces the audience when drawing or writing on the projector surface roll.

Disadvantages   The slides distract attention from the speaker; it is necessary to have a screen or suitable wall on which to project the image.

Prepared visual-aid boards

Boards can be prepared in any size. A popular format is to use the boards on a 'blackboard'-type easel.

Advantages   A highly professional dimension is added to the presentation; it is clear that trouble has been taken in the preparation; visual-aid boards are not used as frequently as other aids.

Disadvantages   The boards require skilled preparation; the cost may be significant; the boards can be bulky to carry around; careful storage is necessary to avoid deterioration.

Samples and models

Advantages   Samples can be passed around the room, involving the sense of touch; samples provide additional interest, and offer examples of actual goods or articles with which the audience is concerned.

Disadvantages Samples and models may need careful preparation.

35mm projector slides, films, video tapes, audio tapes

Advantages Such visual and audio-visual aids add a highly professional element to the presentation; the contents are able to reinforce a presentation of appropriate academic or communications standard.

Disadvantages Preparation of material requires planning, time and expense; there are the possible pitfalls of equipment not functioning or functioning badly; operating audio-visual equipment needs training and practice; the material tends to be a distraction, if not used properly.

Computer graphics

Advantages This aid is modern and up to date and is used with dramatic effect; with appropriate equipment the graphics are relayed on to a large screen.

Disadvantages Computing skill is required, together with the necessary computer hardware.

Photographs

Advantages Photographs are portable, precise and effective.

Disadvantages Depending on the quality selected, the cost factor may intrude.

A SET OF GOLDEN RULES

Question   **What are the 'golden rules' for using visual aids?**

When planning to make use of visual aids there are important dos and don'ts to observe.

- While at a flip chart or board, do not talk with your back to the audience.
- Do not write on a flip chart or board with your back to the audience. Position the board or chart so that you can stand sideways, and look at the audience as soon as the writing or drawing is finished.
- Do not scribble. Take extra time to write clearly.
- Use multiple colours whenever possible.
- Always give titles or headings to anything written.
- Keep aids hidden until required. Remove or erase when finished.
- When a pointer is held do not play with it whilst talking – this is an extremely common failing.
- Write trigger words in pencil on prepared flip-chart sheets. They cannot usually be seen by the audience, but take care not to peer at the chart when reading.
- Always convert statistics and figures into bar charts or pie charts. A mass of figures, whether undifferentiated or complex, extinguishes attention in a matter of seconds.
- Fold the bottom left-hand corner of the first sheet of any prepared flip-chart sheet sequence. This helps easy selection.

PLANNING FOR THE TALKING

Question   **What is the best format for an effective presentation?**

A well-balanced presentation comprises three sections: a beginning, a middle and an end.

The beginning consists of the following.

Welcoming courtesies   The presenter's manner is pleasant, business-like, confident and authoritative. The audience is greeted, and any person who has introduced the presenter is thanked for what he or she has said.

Self-identification   The presenter tells the audience his or her name, experience, areas of knowledge, and the names and status of any colleagues who are assisting in the presentation.

Intentions   The objectives of the presentation are stated. *Example:* Ladies and Gentlemen. It is my intention that by the end of this talk, all present understand how a marketing approach to dental practice offers tangible benefits to both patient and practitioner.

Route map   The route map covers the main points to be explored. It tells how the presentation is to be structured and how long it will last.

In the middle section the current position is stated. Options are considered and proposals are argued.

In the ending, the facts which have been given, the options considered and any proposal made are summarized. The audience is clearly told what action, if any, is to be taken.

Throughout, there are rules to follow.

Rules to follow

- Stand with feet slightly apart in a relaxed manner. Adrenalin is certainly pumping round the presenter's body, but an effort to appear relaxed, must be made.
- Hold hands together, resting lightly on the speaker's stomach. Alternatively, hold the sides of the lectern, if one is used, or hold the prepared notes.
- Do not lean forward to rest hands on a table. The body should be upright.
- Look at the audience, but do not start speaking until there is silence.
- Use the hands to emphasize points of the presentation. The body is an excellent visual aid, when used effectively.
- Tell the audience when questions may be asked.
- Tell the audience if interruptions are welcome or permitted.
- If handouts are provided, advise the audience when it is not necessary for notes to be taken.
- When distributing handouts before the end of a presentation, allow time for reading. Otherwise, instruct the audience to put away the handouts and read them afterwards so that the presentation may continue.
- Do not use jargon, acronyms, slang or bad language.
- Identify and control mannerisms that are likely to irritate or distract the audience. The presenter is unlikely to perceive such mannerisms alone, so intimate friends must be asked to disclose them. A video-taped recording of a trial performance provides a presenter with an excellent opportunity of evaluating presentational skills.

- Use pauses for dramatic emphasis.
- Modulate the voice to sustain interest.
- Ensure that the voice does not drop at the end of a sentence or paragraph. This is a very common failing.
- Maintain continuous eye contact with all the audience. Methodically look from side to side: do not look continuously at the floor, ceiling, or into the middle distance. This is also a very common failing.
- Do not mumble or gabble.

IMPROVEMENT STARTS AT HOME

Question   What self-help action leads to improved performance.

As stated above, a video-taped recording of a presentation is a powerful analytical tool. An audio-taped recording is very useful too, but it does not disclose visual mannerisms which diminish performance.

The following checklist is for use after a presentation has been delivered. It is designed to identify aspects of the presentation that should be improved.

Presentation self-appraisal form

Answer the following questions and place a tick in the appropriate box.

	YES	NO
• Was the venue adequately prepared	☐	☐
• Did my notes contribute to the presentation?	☐	☐
• Did I maintain good eye contact throughout	☐	☐
• Did I control my physical mannerisms?	☐	☐

- Did I use hand gestures effectively?   □   □
- Did I retain audience interest?   □   □
- Am I confident that my voice was well   □   □
  modulated?
- Do I remember using pauses   □   □
  effectively?

If the answers are Yes, OK. If No, do something about it.

SUMMARY

Question What questions should be asked when a presentation is to be made?

Answer The answers to the questions Why? Who? What? How? Where? and When? structure the planning of a presentation.

Question What are the practical aspects of preparing to make a presentation?

Answer The practical aspects of preparing for a presentation are:

- identifying the needs of the target audience;
- writing out the presentation in full;
- timing the script;
- reducing the script to notes of salient points on postcard-sized cards.

Question What kinds of visual aids contribute to a presentation?

Answer Visual aids include blackboards, whiteboards, flip charts, films, audio tapes, video tapes, samples, models, photographs, overhead slide

and 35mm slide projectors, and computer graphics.
The respective benefits of the various aids need to be
weighed against the complexity of preparation and
costs.

**Question   What are the 'golden rules' for using
visual aids?**

Answer   There are ten dos and don'ts in respect of
using visual aids. The most important rules are not to
write or talk with the presenter's back to the audience.

**Question   What is the best format for an effective
presentation?**

Answer   The presentation is structured into three
sections. The beginning commences with welcoming
courtesies, self-identification, intentions and a route
map. In the middle section the current position is
stated, options are considered and proposals argued.
The end section summarizes and states clearly actions
to be followed.

**Question   What self-help action leads to improved
performance?**

Answer   Evaluation of performance through analysis
of a video-taped recording is the most powerful of the
analytical tools. An audio-taped recording is good but
permits no criticism of physical mannerisms. Use of a
self-appraisal form is productive.

7 Selling services

Before reading this chapter try to answer the following questions. The material is worked through in the text. Questions and answers appear together at the end of the chapter by way of summary.

QUESTIONS

What makes buyers buy?

What are the components of the purchase decision-making process?

What simple questioning techniques secure all necessary information?

What format is helpful for selling by telephone?

Chapter 7 synopsis

- Yes please
- The different stages
- Finding out
- A set of rules

YES PLEASE

Question What makes buyers buy?

When a person buys a service he or she sees it as a means to improvement, pleasure or the resolution of a problem. Other factors may intrude, too: sometimes a purchase is made from habit, or even to allay boredom.

But underlying the buyer's feelings, there is a basic mechanism. Buying is a process of satisfying needs. So, for the professional person to sell two categories of action are necessary.

The needs of the buyer are identified

Needs are not straightforward, there are complications. A continuum of need items or activities can start with those which are essential for the survival and continuation of the host or the firm. But along the scale the needs turn into a format more complex and grandiose – they become wants. It is no longer essential for survival or growth that the needs are satisfied; but it is desirable. And wants occur with greater or less intensity, in just the same way that needs are of great or little importance.

Take as an example a sole practitioner solicitor who works with one full-time secretary. The secretary asks for a word-processor to replace the broken office type-writer. A word processor would increase the efficiency of her secretarial output by at least 20 per cent. It is an important need.

The practitioner requires a car to travel from the village where he lives to the busy town where he practises. Without a car travelling takes two hours each way. He wants a Porsche: it is fast, it is full of status. He argues to himself that a Porsche adds credibility to his professional practice. The reality is that a battered Metro could satisfy the transport needs; the desire for the Porsche is a want. In the process of selling, rational buying motives support the satisfaction of the straightforward need. Other factors intrude when it is the potential customer's want that has to be satisfied. The seller has to distinguish between needs and wants to marshall the appropriate service benefits to sell.

The buyer buys

The selling process is complex. The potential buyer is helped to understand how the benefits of the service on offer satisfy his or her needs.

In addition, he or she is motivated to take action – purchasing – so that the benefits do actually satisfy the needs. There are many situations where benefits and needs are precisely matched. The *potential* buyer knows this but does nothing; until the buyer buys, selling has not taken place.

THE DIFFERENT STAGES

Questions **What are the components of the purchase decision-making process?**

It is important to know how buyers think. If the individual elements of the purchase decision-making process are known, they can be manipulated. Skilful selling achieves control – with appropriate techniques people are moved or motivated to change from a state of total non-interest to a decision to buy. Table 7.1 illustrates the sequence of stages in a buying decision.

Table 7.1
The sequence of stages in a buying decision

Buyer's thoughts/feelings	Stage
I am me. Respect me.	1 No interest
What is this I see?	2 Casual interest
Do I need it? Do I want it?	3 Motivated interest
Shall I search for something different?	4 Shopping comparisons
Where can I buy what I need?	5 Selection commitment
I am going to buy. I feel good.	6 *Buying decision*
Oh dear! Did I make the right decision?	7 Post-purchase doubts

Professional salespeople, good at their job, can move a potential customer through all the stages from non-interest to buying. This may take place at one meeting or over a period of time, depending on the profession. Success is not achieved every time, but the better the salesperson the more often he or she succeeds. There is no reason why every professional person cannot learn to sell effectively. The calibre of the selling techniques must harmonize with the dignity of the particular profession.

Table 7.2 shows the sales techniques necessary to move a prospective buyer through the successive stages.

Sales techniques

Attention getting

Initial contact is courteous and polite. The successful salesperson is careful to see that he or she speaks well

Table 7.2
Sales techniques needed at each stage

Stage		Sales technique
1	No interest	Attention getting
2	Casual interest	
		Qualifying through questions
3	Motivated interest	The sales presentation
4	Shopping comparisons	Objection handling
5	Selection commitment	Benefit messages; trial close
6	*Buying decision*	The close
7	Post-purchase doubts	Reinforcement benefit messages

and is well groomed. He or she presents both the image of his or her company and him or herself in a manner designed to impress and be remembered. Any pre-established bonds that exist from other contacts or meetings, are used. Charm, personal attributes and experience are all concentrated on the effort of grasping and holding the attention of the buyer.

Qualifying through questions

The salesperson probes to identify the potential buyer's real needs. With skilful use of open, closed and leading questions, he or she can find out almost anything. When the needs are known, the presentation is tailored to match those needs as closely as possible to the benefit functions of the service.

The sales presentation

An effective presentation describes, highlights, simplifies and magnifies everything the service gives to the buyer who buys. The sales presentation is an ordered sequence of description and promise. It uses words or demonstration, touch or sound, taste or smell or visual reinforcement to communicate benefits to the potential buyer. Sometimes one only, sometimes many of these factors are used. Those qualities of the service, that is, the service benefits nearest to the client's wants and needs, are singled out.

For example, the optician reinforces the value of tri-focal lenses to the art historian. In the course of the historian's work, many paintings displayed on walls have to be looked at. Because of weak middle-distance vision the art historian has to peer at paintings, either close to or from a particular distance. The optician sells the benefit of tri-focal lenses – providing 'normal' vision without the need to peer.

The benefit function is singled out to match an identified individual need. The tri-focal spectacles, made with plastic lenses, have other benefit features such as lightness and economy. But the selling impact of these benefits is not as great.

Objection handling

There are many reasons why people do not buy – insufficient money, lack of authority, inadequate knowledge of the service benefits, fear of making a decision. Sometimes it is simply inertia.

If a salesperson is to close a sale, he or she must overcome all the objections. The objection that is given is not always the real objection.

'No thank you. Just a haircut please. I am playing squash in an hour's time and the shampoo would be wasted.' An acceptable reason is given to the barber. Really, the young man does not want to pay the extra cost of the shampoo service. Neither does he wish to admit that expense is the reason for declining the offer.

In the case of a service with a very small unit cost, such as a shampoo, the seller does not try to overcome the objection: a valid or even artificial reason is accepted.

It is a different matter when the stakes are higher. The seller has to find out what the real objection is, and then produce persuasive argument, sandwiched between cogent service benefits, why the service should be accepted.

There are different styles of objection handling.

The throwback method   The objection itself is used as a selling point. For example:

'No thank you. The service is too expensive.'

'It is good that you have considered the fee costs. They are our guarantee of reliability and professionalism. We have committed ourselves to a reputation of quality and concern, and this is reflected by our fees. Please ask any of our clients.'

Comparison with competitive service   The benefits are compared with those of the competition. The carefully chosen example shows the competition at a real disadvantage. For instance:

'Our domestic tree surgery service includes felling, lopping, grading and stacking. Selected timber is stored so that it dries and can be used as firewood. We believe that householders should enjoy all the benefits of their dead timbers.'

The lock close   This is a very powerful way of meeting an objection. It counters the objection and then closes at the same time. The commitment of the prospective client is obtained, on condition that the objection is shown to be unfounded. For example:

'No thank you. I did not want just the rail tickets. I need to stay at the conference hotel overnight.'

'That is no problem. If I can arrange an inclusive rail/hotel accommodation package for you may we book your reservations?'

Another effective technique is to repeat the objection to the person who has made it. It gives time to think. The potential client then hears the objection out of context with what has been said, and sometimes this diminishes its impact.

The question is then asked: 'Is that the only objection?'

On no account does the seller argue. Even if the prospective client's objection is highly contentious the seller deals with the matter circumspectly. 'Yes. But . . .' is an effective method – 'Well I see how you view the situation. But have you considered . . . ?'

Benefit messages

The benefit message is a statement of what the service can do for the client. It gives hope, and promise; it gives answers. But it is important in formulating the benefit message that the function of the benefit is described, not the specification of how the service is delivered.

In the process of selling, benefit messages are used in two ways.

Introductory benefit statements   The benefit feature of the service is introduced and described, in a straightforward manner without undue emphasis.

Closing benefit statement   The benefit features are enlarged, expanded and heightened in order specifically to move the client to making a decision to purchase.

An example of an introductory benefit statement would be: 'The Sinclair QL microcomputer has four programs. Quill is the word-processing program.

Compare a closing benefit statement: 'The Quill program of the Sinclair QL microcomputer is an easy-to-use word-processing program. Because Quill is simple, and is accompanied by a clearly set out instruction manual, beginners are able to print out business letters in a very short time.'

Trial close

Throughout a sales presentation a good salesperson continuously solicits indications that he or she is moving in the right direction. 'Will it help?' 'What contribution will it make to your cash flow?' 'Do you think that that is a good idea?'

Every 'Yes' that is given reinforces the move towards a final close. If the question receives a 'No' response, the salesperson must consolidate his or her position. The trial close is a method of testing the water, without placing the salesperson in a position from which it is difficult to recover.

The close

A sale is achieved when a presentation is closed successfully. There are a number of closes although not many are used: the close that was effective last time is often used.

The direct close   The person selling asks directly for the order. This is a very strong close, perhaps the strongest of all. It is of paramount importance that, when this close is used, the seller does not say another word after asking for instructions. The first person to speak loses. The longer the silence after a request for an order, the more difficult it is for the client to say 'No'.

Weak salespeople crumble when they ask directly for an order. Because they worry that the answer is going to be 'No', and the order lost, they follow up with additional benefits – 'May we print the brochure for you?' and then, instead of silence, add 'The combination of those three colours is very eye-catching.' The moment additional words are spoken the buyer is let off the hook; the pressure is removed. He or she has been given the opportunity to talk about the benefit statement, instead of making a decision.

The indirect assumptive close A formal request for order instructions is not made; instead, a simple question is asked relating to a minor detail. But the implication of the question is that a decision to proceed has already been made.

For example: 'Do you want us to supply all the audio-visual equipment for the training sessions?'

The indirect alternative close The client is given two secondary service alternatives to choose from. The real issue as to whether the service itself is to be selected is sidestepped, so the importance of the decision the buyer has to make is psychologically reduced.

Examples of this type of close are:

- 'Would you prefer to settle the fee account by cash or cheque.'
- 'Is the work to be carried out in the morning or the afternoon?'
- 'Would the staff prefer the scheme with profits or without?'

Concession close Granting concessions and discounts to close business is weak selling. Concessions are sometimes appropriate because, without, a contract is not placed. But it should be the exception; and concessions are most effective when made available at the end of the presentation. The impact of the concession as a concession is lost at the beginning. It assumes merely the role of an introductory benefit statement. Concessions take a number of forms:

- discounted fees, costs or premiums;
- extended payment terms;
- free after-sales service;
- free maintenance period;
- free installation;
- free training;

and there are many others.

Concession selling is an attitude of mind. There are those who privately believe that without granting discounts and concessions business development is an uphill task. In such situations the erosion of net profit is often overlooked.

There is a question to ask when tempted to offer a discount. By how much must turnover increase at the discounted fee rate, or discounted price, to sustain the same margin of profit?

Table 7.3 provides figures illustrating the sales increases necessary at certain discount levels.

Table 7.3
Increase in sales volume percentage necessary to maintain gross profit when discounting prices

Price reduction	Gross profit margin		
	60%	50%	30%
5%	9%	11%	20%
10%	20%	25%	50%
15%	33%	43%	100%
20%	50%	67%	200%

$$\text{Volume increase \%} = \frac{\text{Price reduction} \times 100}{\text{New gross profit margin}}$$

The plus and minus method   To reach a buying decision a client mentally tots up the negative and positive attributes of the service being offered. If the seller fulfils his

or her function successfully, all the minuses will have
been neutralized – some will even have been converted
to pluses.

But until the buyer reaches the buying decision, his
or her thinking may not be clear cut. The plus and
minus close is the seller's attempt to offer clarification,
albeit structured towards an order being placed:

'Mr Freeman, we have discussed your company's
needs and what our services can do to help. I know you
are in the process of arriving at a decision. Whilst our
service has many positive features – and I hope I have
explained them all to you fully – there are also certain
objections. Frankly, although I would very much like to
have your instructions, I would rather withdraw now
than have you commit your firm to a decision that is not
absolutely right. Look, I have a suggestion. In order to
clarify the situation let us compare the pros and cons.'
The client is then handed a sheet of paper and a pen.

'On the left-hand side of this sheet, please write down
all the advantages accruing to your company in
employing our services. On the right-hand side list all
the reasons against.'

The seller works hard to help the client think of every
possible advantage. The seller says nothing about the
disadvantages of using the service. Consequently, the list
of pluses is much longer.

'The next step, Mr Freeman, is to count the items in
the columns. There are twenty-one items for – and eight
items against. That really makes the decision for you,
Mr Freeman. It is definitely the correct decision to give
us your instructions.'

The halo effect close   In this type of close, use is made
of the halo effect of prestigious clients. The prospective
client is encouraged to copy the buying decisions made
by organizations of comparable or greater substance. In

this way the threat of making a wrong decision is felt to be reduced. For example:

'Well, I am not convinced that this pension plan format is right for my staff.'

'Yes, it is a difficult decision. It is one that faced British Airways too. But I am happy to say that having decided to go ahead, last year, it has met an enthusiastic reception from their staff.'

FINDING OUT

Questions **What simple questioning techniques secure all necessary information?**

Qualifying through questions

The salesperson probes to identify the potential buyer's real needs. With skilful use of questions, he or she can find out almost anything. The following questions are all that are needed.

The neutral closed question

This invites a 'Yes' or 'No' answer. It elicits a short factual reply:

- 'Do you act for overseas clients?'
- 'Have you ever had difficulty in seeing at night?'
- 'Have you ever seen an electronic measuring rule?'

The neutral closed question is often used to launch a fact-finding enquiry using the range of questions. It does not by itself invite an elaborate reply, but it is very useful in identifying or eliminating subject areas so that further questions may follow: 'Do you act for overseas clients?'
'No.'

'Would you be interested in working with Canadian engineers?'
'Yes.'
'We have offices in . . .'
Neutral closed questions usually begin with:

- 'Would you . . . ?'
- 'Do you . . . ?'
- 'Can you . . . ?'

The neutral open question

The objective of the neutral open question is to obtain a lot of information. The form of the reply is deliberately not structured by the questioner. No matter how comprehensive the answer, the information given is only as much as the person wants to give.
Examples of such questions are:

- 'What are the factors that influence your decision?'
- 'Why was the meeting postponed?'
- 'How was he trained?'

The neutral leading question

The questioner sets the scene. Limits are imposed on the answer that is given. The person who gives the answer has the freedom to make any reply but the parameters of the questions limit the response within a particular range.
Neutral leading questions usually start with the words 'When . . . ?' 'Who . . . ?' or 'Where . . . ?'
Examples of these are:

- 'When did you discover that the assistant was ill?'
- 'Who is responsible for this mess?'
- 'Where did he put the research figures?'

The neutral closed, open and leading questions are all that are required. There are two other questions with a more specialized application.

The loaded minus question

The questioner strongly influences the reply in a negative context. The loaded minus question starts with:

- 'You wouldn't . . .'
- 'You don't . . .'
- 'You haven't . . .'

The person asking the question also shakes his or her head while speaking, so that the person being questioned is led, very strongly, to produce a negative answer. For example:

- 'You don't think, in the circumstances, that we ought to act for them, do you?'
- 'You haven't suggested that we transgress the guidelines of the Institute, have you?'

The loaded plus question

Similar to the neutral leading question, the loaded plus question guides the answer which is obtained. The questioner puts his or her question in a complimentary and respectful framework. Flattery will also be present. The person replying needs effort and a strong will to move away from the direction that has been set.

Examples would include:

- 'Mr Councillor, you have had years of experience of making this type of arrangement. You do agree that it is the best sequence of events, don't you?'
- 'Mr Brunswick, you are by far the most photo-genic in the group. You do agree that you should

be the one to face the television cameras, don't you?'

When the needs are known, the presentation is tailored to match those needs as closely as possible with the benefit functions of the service.

It is often helpful to plan in advance how to identify the client's needs. The following brief checklist will help.

Checklist

- What is the information required?
- What are the questions that will get the information quickly?
- What are the best neutral open questions to use?
- What answers am I expecting to receive?
- What questions can identify the full range of their interests?

A SET OF RULES

Questions   **What format is helpful for selling by telephone?**

In some professions direct sales contact with potential clients is not yet permitted, even where the approach has restraint and dignity. But values are changing. At the appropriate time, there are working rules to facilitate prospecting for business by phone.

Working rules 1 to 5

Working rule 1   Identify the existing main categories of client segment. Select prospective clients to approach from within these groupings. Prepare a simple three-column grid and enter the main client categories in the first column

Figure 7.1 illustrates the format of the grid – a prospecting grid – mentioned in rule 1.

The objective is to eliminate contact with potential clients for whom there is no possibility of acting. In Figure 7.1 six categories are shown. Depending on the profession, the number can be five or seven or any other.

Working rule 2   Identify sources of names and addresses of prospective clients falling within the main client categories. Enter the reference sources in the middle column of the prospecting grid

Names and addresses of corporate clients are published in one directory or another. Alternatively, the names of companies appear in journals, newspapers, registers or the trade press. If a company is anonymous to the extent that its name cannot be found in published form, it is unlikely that it qualifies as a potential client. Most businesses advertise themselves, if only by a line entry in a directory.

The directory giving the most detailed information is *Kompass* published by Kompass Publishers Ltd, Windsor Court, East Grinstead House, East Grinstead, West Sussex RH19 1XD: telephone 0342 26972; telex 95127 INFSER G. It segments its data against many criteria – product type, distribution channels, turnover, resources employed, geographical location and so on.

Yellow pages   This, the most readily available directory, is also helpful. If the prospective clients are private persons, the electoral rolls supply names and addresses.

PROSPECT   WHERE FOUND   PROSPECT NEEDS
CATEGORIES

1. _____

2. _____

3. _____

4. _____

5. _____

6. _____

Figure 7.1   A prospecting grid

Working rule 3   Identify the principal needs of the different prospective client categories. Enter the needs in column 3 of the prospecting grid

When contact is made cold, it is essential to discuss matters of interest to the potential client. Otherwise the client's attention span may be very short.

Working rule 4   Identify the primary and secondary objectives to be achieved

A professional firm is often able to provide many services. When telephoning cold, it is necessary to identify the potential client's needs at an early stage. This is achieved through questioning. Appropriate service benefits are then given to match such needs. For example, Computer Training and Consultancy Ltd telephones a local printing firm. The sequence to be followed is:

- the prospective client is dialled;
- contact is made with the manager or proprietor;
- caller introduces self and company;
- caller obtains basic details of the prospective client:
  - to ensure that the conversation is with a decision-maker;
  - to identify whether the firm uses computers, intends to use computers in the future, or does not see a need for computer application;
- benefits are offered;
- client objections are countered;
- a meeting is arranged;
- in the face of a declined meeting, the potential client is advised that literature is being sent, with a subsequent follow-up telephone call.

Working rule 5   A script for the prospecting call is written, in the form of an algorithm, making sure that the 'Golden rules for speaking on the telephone' are employed

Golden rules

Golden rule 1   Always smile when picking up the receiver

Smiling is consciously relaxing. A friendly, courteous smile communicates itself to the other end of the phone.

Golden rule 2   Involve the prospective client in conversation as early as possible

At all costs the client must not be talked at. If the telephone has to be held away at arm's length to avoid a deluge of words pouring out, the objective is never going to be reached.

Golden rule 3   Ask frequent questions

The caller is ensuring that the client qualifies as a prospect. At the same time the client is brought into the conversation.

Golden rule 4   The prospective client listens only as long as he or she is interested

A detailed description of the caller's professional skills and successes is not necessarily of interest, neither is an observation on the weather or the success of the local cricket club. Many people are courteous, but this is not a licence to ramble on. The caller's objective can only be achieved when the caller has the client's full attention. Attention is given, although not always, when client needs and wants are being discussed.

Golden rule 5   Always aim at achieving the objectives

A pleasant easy conversation does not secure a sale by itself. There must be control at all times, moving in a planned way towards the objectives. At the telephone, not a second must be wasted – every word and every question must contribute to reaching the desired goal.

Golden rule 6   When the client says 'No' start selling

'No' is an objection to be overcome. The drive towards achieving the objective is continued. 'No' might take the form of:

- 'Not now . . .'
- Business is bad . . .'
- 'There is no budget for . . .'

The objections may be a smoke-screen to hide other reasons for not buying. But 'No' is not a signal for the caller to say 'Thank you for listening' and to put the telephone down. It is a signal that the caller must redouble his or her efforts to identify the real needs of the customer – and to match them with appropriate benefits.

Figure 7.2 gives an example of a prospecting script showing individual blocs within the conversation and the alternative response directions.

The telephone script is the plan allowing the caller to lead the client to the fulfilment of the objective. The client does not know that he or she is being led. The script endeavours to predict every response from the client which is likely to be met. The original script is often amended, after a call has generated a different or unexpected client reaction.

Callers experienced in selling by telephone still make use of a script. It is a valuable control mechanism to

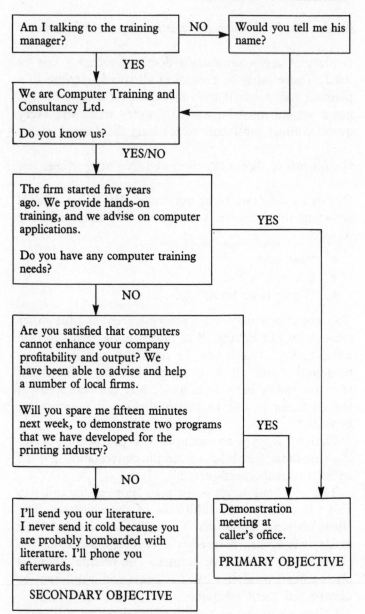

Figure 7.2   A prospecting script

prevent the conversation going off at an unproductive tangent.

Working rules 6 to 9

Working rule 6   Prepare and maintain a simple record system to enter all prospecting calls made

Figure 7.3 illustrates the format of index card or exercise book for keeping records of prospecting calls.

Every prospective client lead is valuable. If a prospective client is called and he or she is not in, the call must be made again later. If the caller does not bother, but simply moves on to the next name and address, sooner or later the supply of available leads dries up. It is tempting and easier just to move on; it is also much less bother to leave out the names and addresses and the

Contact name	Company name	Telephone number	Prospect address	Action

Keeping a record of all calls made is almost as important as the nature of the prospecting call script itself. Prospecting is an extremely effective method of securing business.

The records that are kept should be simple.

An index card or exercise book is all that is required

Figure 7.3   A record of prospecting calls

'action' column details. The temptation lies in thinking that every detail is going to be remembered – memory is unreliable and a written record is essential.

If a message is given to the caller that the client is out but will be in his or her office on Tuesday at tea-time, then that is the time the second call must be made. Whatever instructions are given to the caller, they must be entered in the 'Action' column.

Every day the index card is looked through to see which call-backs are to be made.

Working rule 7   Whenever possible telephone in the afternoon when calls are cheaper. Identify by experience and by trial and error the best times of day to telephone different client categories

There is no set time to call. Given that there are differential costs in respect of the time of day when a call is made, when there is a reason for calling, call. Prospecting for business by telephone is an activity which must also fit into the caller's own practice timetable. There are often free minutes during the day which should be used, as long as they fit into a planned programme of prospecting.

Working rule 8   Decide on a target number of prospecting calls for a week's trial period. Draw a target record grid and enter the target number of calls with objectives to be met, set against performance results.

Telephone prospecting is a cost-effective marketing tool. Positive results are achieved if the activity is carried out skilfully. Inexperience limits performance. It is important at the beginning of a telephone prospecting campaign that the target set is realistic. If the target is too ambitious it is not reached. Failure to meet one's own target is a strong demotivator. If this is allowed to happen it is tempting to discard the entire activity as non-productive – which need not be the case.

Working rule 9   Make use of the prospecting letter as a crutch at the beginning of a telephone prospecting campaign

Many people, good at selling face to face, balk at attempting to sell by telephone. There are no easily discernible non-verbal signals to interpret. Sending a prospecting letter before telephoning greatly simplifies the task. The caller is following up a letter and uncertainty is reduced. The experience then presents few difficulties.

Prospecting by letter with a follow-up telephone call is less cost-effective than prospecting by telephone alone. But psychologically the combination of letter and telephone is supportive. It is useful to start with the two activities, weaning oneself from the prospecting letter as experience grows.

SUMMARY

Questions   **What makes buyers buy?**

Answer   Buyers buy a service as a method of improving pleasure or to resolve a problem.

Question   **What are the components of the purchase decision-making process?**

Answer   There are seven stages in the purchase decision-making process: no interest, casual interest, motivated interest, shopping comparisons, selection commitment, the buying decision and post-purchase doubts.

Question **What simple questioning techniques secure all necessary information?**

Answer There are three groups of question to ask to obtain information: neutral closed, neutral open and neutral leading questions. In addition, loaded plus and loaded minus questions help to manipulate the answers that are given.

Question **What format is helpful for selling by telephone?**

Answer There is a set of operating rules to structure telephone selling. For speaking on the telephone the 'Golden rules' apply.

8   Negotiating to win

Before reading this chapter try to answer the following questions. The material is worked through in the text. Questions and answers appear together at the end of the chapter by way of a summary.

QUESTIONS

What is the difference between negotiating and selling?

What are the basic steps in the negotiating process?

What practical tasks help the negotiator prepare to enter the negotiating arena?

What is the best way to open negotiations?

What tactical options are open to negotiators?

What are the nuts and bolts of negotiation?

What are the 'golden rules of bargaining'?

Chapter 8 synopsis

- Definition
- The structure of negotiation
- Getting ready
- How to begin
- Different ways to go
- Tactics
- Core elements
- A set of rules

DEFINITION

Question What is the difference between negotiating and selling?

In a commercially orientated environment where services are sold the seller's objective is to conclude a sale. A buyer buys a service; a deal is struck. Depending on the seller's skill, the buyer is moved from a state of non-interest, or partial interest, to the point where a purchase commitment is made.

In terms of positive movement of both parties, the buyer is stationary, the seller is flexible. There is a little reactive movement from the buyer, but what there is seeks either to move closer to the buyer or to try to escape. Figure 8.1 shows this diagrammatically.

Negotiation is different, there is movement on both sides. Both parties are moving towards each other, attempting to conclude a deal; both sides are flexible. The mechanism of negotiation is a trading of concessions

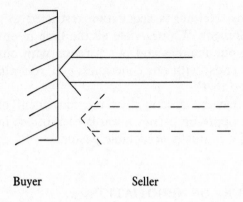

Buyer   Seller

The sales situation

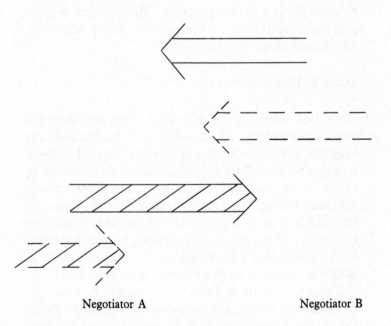

Negotiator A   Negotiator B

The negotiation

Figure 8.1   The difference between selling and negotiating

and propositions. Neither is negotiation restricted to a business environment. We negotiate all the time in our daily life: with our families and our parents; with our children and friends; with our colleagues – 'If you will do this, I will do that!'

Negotiation may be described as the movement of independent or opposing parties towards each other, in the direction of a mutually acceptable position.

THE STRUCTURE OF NEGOTIATION

Question **What are the basic steps in the negotiating process?**

Negotiation is a planned activity. The essential ingredients are what has to be achieved, how, and at what cost. The negotiation steps are:

Stage 1: Preparation

Objectives are not necessarily fixed; there are upper and lower limits within which a deal may be reached. For example, party A is a seller of services, party B a buyer. A considers that the value of service X, as measured by the fee to be paid, is £100 per hour, but is not entirely sure that service X is exactly what B is going to accept. Possibly X–1 or X–2 is the service that exactly matches B's needs, or purse. So in preparing to negotiate with B, A decides that a fee range of £80 to £100 reflects an equitable fee for a service ranging from X to X–2.

A wants to settle at £100, but is willing to enter into an agreement at any point between £80 and £100. Below £80 – the lower limit – A is not prepared to reach agreement.

What does B really want? If A successfully predicts

£80   £90   £100 per hour

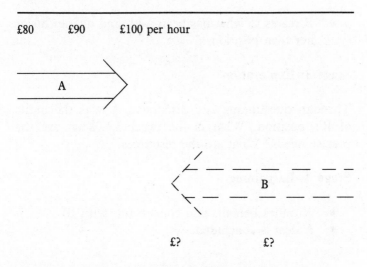

Figure 8.2   Party A opens with £100 per hour: party B reacts with a lower counter-offer

what B wants A can test that objective during negotiations. Waiting until B states a position from the negotiating arena is too late. Possibly B's opening statements
are bluff?

Stage 2: Confrontation

A projects how B is going to react to the opening
position. A searches to find any indicators from reputation, or past experience, of how B is likely to respond
to A's demand. It is reasonable to assume that for B
there are also upper and lower limits at which agreement
can be reached.

   Figure 8.2 shows the projected position of the two
parties at the commencement of negotiations.

- A's position is stated – service is offered at £100
  per hour.

- B reacts to what has been said, and defines his or her own position.

Stage 3: Exploration

Through questioning and discussion A tests the limits of B's position. What is the urgency? What are the precise needs? What are the resources?

Stage 4: Bargaining

- A trades benefits and concessions with B.
- A deal is concluded.

GETTING READY

Question   **What practical tasks help the negotiator prepare to enter the negotiating arena?**

Before giving an operatic performance, the professional opera singer practises his or her scales. The boxer limbers up. Negotiation is no different: there is training and rehearsal. The following checklist gives a structure for the preparation for negotiation.

Checklist: Negotiation planning

- What are our objectives, in terms of marketing/selling/service production/finance/personnel/technology?
- What are the other side's objectives?
- Predict the upper and lower limits of both sides' objectives.
- If the other party is part of a distribution chain, what are the related end-user needs?
- On which elements is the other side likely to nego-

tiate – fees, service quality, volume, technical support, delivery, credit, guarantee, resources?

- Which of the elements is going to be negotiated most keenly? Why?
- Taking each element in turn, what concessions are wanted?
- What concessions do we want in return?
- What is the financial cost of the different concessions?
- What is the value (non-financial) of those concessions?
- Which concessions from us are most valuable to the other side – and vice versa?
- Which concessions have the most value but cost the least?
- Taking all possible concessions into account, how much money is involved?
- What stance is the other side likely to adopt at the first meeting?
- Given our best estimate of the other side's requirements, and our objectives, how far apart are we?
- What common ground is there between us?
- What sequence do we want the negotiations to follow?
- Have we the psychological advantage of meeting at our offices?
- Who is to represent us? What is their brief?

HOW TO BEGIN

Question **What is the best way to open negotiations?**

Negotiations should start realistically, but caution is appropriate too.

To take an example, when the Beatles became famous,

it happened rather quickly. The Beatles' manager, Brian Epstein, realized that there was money to be made from the sale of premium goods – T-shirts, ash trays, pens, mugs, hold-alls. All would have the Beatles' logo.

He made contact with the largest premium-goods manufacturer he could find, with an invitation to negotiate a deal. When they called at his office, Brian Epstein thumped his office desk and said, 'The Beatles are the hottest property on the pop scene at the moment. We would like you to manufacture and market a range of Beatles premium goods. But there is no way', he said, 'that we would accept less than 7.5 per cent royalty from your quoted prices.'

The manufacturers argued and tried to negotiate, but in the end they settled at the figure. This meant that they went away, manufactured, marketed and sold the goods. From all the money they collected, they gave 7.5 per cent to the Beatles.

Subsequently, much later, they disclosed to a third party that when they had gone to Epstein's office, they had expected to have to give away 50 per cent of their takings.

Brian Epstein generated substantial cash for the Beatles without prior investment. Many try to emulate this success. Perhaps, with a different approach to negotiation, the sum could have been larger. The opening did not make provision for establishing the negotiating strengths of the other side.

DIFFERENT WAYS TO GO

Question   **What tactical options are open to negotiators?**

There are many pathways a negotiator can tread. Indeed,

preparation time is well spent in predicting reactions to
opening and succeeding moves. There will sometimes be
historical precedent for the way in which a company
negotiates. Professional negotiators have long memories
– as part of their stock in trade. An opening demand of
19 per cent that settles for 3 per cent one year belies
negotiating strength in another.

There are three main approaches to negotiation.

'Honest Joe' negotiations

The firm is reputable, with a solid track record. The
approach continues: 'We have skills we are willing to
provide in return for a fair fee. The matter is complex,
but application and energy can overcome detail problems. If we cannot find an equitable solution we
shouldn't be in practice.'

Reinforced negotiations

Efforts are made to enhance the perceived image of negotiating strengths. Conversation and attitude combine to
neutralize and extinguish all doubt. Track-record experience is publicized and third parties are lobbied to give
recommendations. The pay-off period is described from
the perspective of small time units, such as the cost
being equivalent to only a packet of cigarettes a day.
Obligations are minimized and sandwiched between
benefit functions. A typical example would be: 'It is
clearly a profitable operation for you. The hire period is
for two years, giving the security of semi-permanent
ownership.'

Creative negotiations

Subordinate actions and pressures are employed to manipulate the reaction of the other side.

For example, two chartered accountants were in business together operating cigarette-vending machines. Out of the blue, one of their cigarette suppliers made an offer to purchase the business. Fortuitously, three days later another of their suppliers indicated an interest in the concern. Thereafter, the two partners were never available together. Their tactic was: 'I am sorry, my partner had to fly to New York. We are in touch by phone. I'll keep our meeting with you and discuss proposals with him afterwards.'

Using this tactic, and playing one buyer off against the other, the partners always made time for leisured consideration of the other sides' offers. They sold their business for three times what they thought it was worth.

There is always room for creativity and originality in negotiation. When a negotiation is concluded both parties should feel that they have reached a good agreement. It is important to remember that the other side do not know how you think and plan. Their expectations are influenced by what you tell them and what you do. You are totally familiar with the resources, the fee levels and the constraints of your practice; but the other side are not. They may try to guess and predict, in just the same way as you endeavour to plot their actions and reactions.

So, if the effort is made to engineer their expectations it can be productive. Take for example the 'tough guy, good guy' tactic.

One member of the negotiating team is aggressive, abrasive, demanding and assertive. His demands are loud and forceful. Another member of the team is very different. 'Look,' he says, 'I am sorry about my

colleague. He is very inflexible and demanding. If we
can discuss this matter quietly I am sure we can reach
agreement, despite what he says. As long as you can
provide . . .'

CORE ELEMENTS

Question **What are the nuts and bolts of
negotiation?**

Negotiation is trading concessions – giving something
away in exchange for something granted in return. Variables are the nuts of negotiation; bolts are the conditions
that are set. A negotiator's resources are made up of
variable and fixed resources.

Without conscious effort, perception of one's
resources does not change. Money and specifications, for
example, are thought of as variables – they always
change. Professional skills or personnel employed are
fixed resources. To change them requires application and
effort.

Negotiation is made easier when there is a plentiful
supply of variables with which to trade. Variables can
be magnified, diminished or subdivided, thus creating a
wider range of variables. For example, fee payments are
demanded promptly, or after thirty, sixty or ninety days.
Alternatively, they remain constant for the first cycle,
with a percentage increment for the second and
subsequent cycles.

Before negotiations commence it is productive to
consider variables and constants carefully. How many
constants can be converted to potential variables? For
example, a firm's capacity for consultancy is limited by
the complement of four skilled engineers on the permanent staff. With effort, the constraint can be lifted,
turning a constant into a variable.

Granting variables is part of the negotiation cycle: receiving them is another. But demand for the variables required has to be presented in a firm, authoritative manner. Variables that are wanted from the other side are classified as conditions – without certain conditions being met negotiations founder. Preparation for negotiation involves identifying required conditions as well as creating variables for exchange. In discussion the conditions are always stated first, for example 'If you supply a full set of working drawings we will prepare a cost schedule for the proposed alterations.'

The pattern of negotiations between parties is the thrust and parry of two fencers. Party A tests the defences of party B with an exploratory thrust – how B reacts influences the intensity and nature of A's second thrust. So every negotiation move is part of a considered plan. Before granting a concession to the other side in response to a thrust, it is necessary to consider:

- What is the value to the other side?
- What is the cost?
- What is wanted in exchange?

A SET OF RULES

Question   What are the 'golden rules of bargaining'?

Bargaining is a skill. If it is not inherited, it can be learned. Bargaining is trading concessions, whether in the boardroom or in the street.

Golden rule 1   Open cautiously

*Golden rule 2   Never reject a proposal without offering an
alternative*

A counter-proposal is an invitation for negotiations to
continue. A flat 'No' necessitates a further exploratory
thrust from the first party. It denies movement. The
negotiator may not know how to progress if the rejection
occurs at an early point.

*Golden rule 3   Make every concession conditional upon
receiving something in return*

Bargaining is a precise activity; it is trading X in return
for Y. A natural response to an acceptable offer is simply
to agree, but tough bargaining achieves more than reactive bargaining. However, there is a real-life problem
which intrudes: most of us want to be liked. Being tough
and always insisting on something in return will threaten
the position. The temptation to worry about how the
other side is viewing the negotiator as a person must be
resisted.

To give an example: 'We are not accustomed to
reducing our fees. But we will agree to your request in
this instance, to initiate a relationship, if you will invite
us to tender for the parallel contract next month.'

*Golden rule 4   When attacking split the other side's
proposals and negotiate component requirements separately.
When defending always link every disputed point before
granting concessions*

Seven parts of a proposal, negotiated separately, result
in the trading of seven sets of concessions. The sum total
of all agreed concessions given away is invariably greater
than the final negotiated settlement of one issue made
up of seven linked points.

Figures 8.3a and 8.3b illustrate the process. In Figure 8.3a each point represents one aspect initially unacceptable to the other side. Depending on the negotiator's skill, greater or lesser concessions are made to reach agreement each time. The shaded portions represent the cost of concessions allowed in order to reach final agreement.

In Figure 8.3b all issues are linked together. The total concessions necessary to reach agreement are seen in relation to the full spectrum of issues. That is a significant difference. When subordinate issues are negotiated singly, there is not necessarily any indication of what further demands may subsequently be made.

When defending, the strategy is to insist on receiving the other side's shopping list. Sometimes it has to be prised away: confidence, authority and persistence may be required to overcome resistance.

For example: 'I can understand that you wish to discuss the nature of the chemical analysis. This we will gladly do because it is essential that our service matches your specification precisely. But what other areas for discussion stand in the way of our helping you? Is chemical analysis the only point at issue?'

Golden rule 5   Opening concessions should be small rather than large

It is very easy to give away more: it is difficult to retrieve a position already conceded. A positive concession, although small, indicates that you are offering movement towards settlement.

Golden rule 6   Never accept the other side's opening offer

It is unlikely that the other side's best position is given in the opening stance. If they, too, obey golden rule 4,

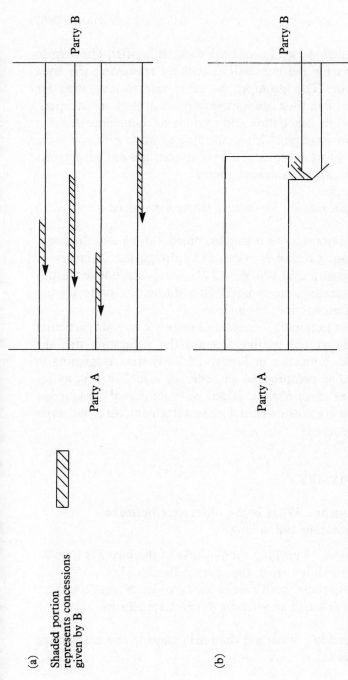

(a)

Shaded portion
represents concessions
given by B

(b)

Figure 8.3 A's demands are (a) negotiated separately; (b) first all linked together

Party B

Party A

Party B

Party A

concessions are being held back. It is often effective to probe for the concessions without specifying the level sought. This prompts the other side to give away far more than they need, especially when they are inexperienced in negotiation and anxious to conclude a deal.

For example: 'We would like to work with you if we can, but the terms you have quoted are not acceptable. How can you improve them?'

Golden rule 7   Summarize the position periodically

It is important to maintain control throughout the negotiation. Control is reinforced through the summary of the position as you see it. Misinterpretations or misunderstandings are avoided. In addition, the summary can be used to move for a close.

For example, ' . . . and in response to your particular needs we are putting forward the suggestion that the work commence in January. Clearly we are agreeing to a major compromise in order to establish a basis for future co-operation. Based on your stated programme there are now no obstacles to agreement. Are you ready to proceed?'

SUMMARY

Question   **What is the difference between negotiating and selling?**

Answer   In selling the position of the buyer is usually fixed, while that of the seller is flexible. In negotiations, both parties are flexible, moving towards each other in an attempt to reach agreement.

Question   **What are the basic steps in the negotiating process?**

Answer The negotiating steps are:

- preparation – setting objectives, projecting the reactions of the other party;
- confrontation – presenting a considered position;
- exploration – testing the other side's reaction and intentions;
- bargaining – trading concessions to reach agreement.

Question **What practical tasks help the negotiator prepare to enter the negotiating arena?**

Answer A prepared checklist assists in the planning and development of a negotiation stance.

Question **What is the best way to open negotiations?**

Answer Negotiations should start realistically and cautiously.

Question **What tactical options are open to negotiators?**

Answer There are three main approaches to negotiations:

- 'Honest Joe' negotiations – reputable, solid, straightforward;
- reinforced negotiations – the perceived offer is constructively enhanced;
- creative negotiations – effort is made to manipulate reactions.

Question **What are the nuts and bolts of negotiation?**

Answer The core elements of negotiation are the

conditions that are stipulated and the concessions traded in the negotiating arena.

Question   What are the 'golden rules of bargaining'?

Answer   The 'golden rules of bargaining' are:

- open cautiously;
- never reject a proposal without offering an alternative;
- make every concession conditional upon receiving something in return;
- when attacking split the other side's proposals and negotiate component requirements separately; when defending always link every disputed point before granting concessions;
- opening concessions should be small rather than large;
- never accept the other side's opening offer;
- summarize the position periodically.

9 Marketing training

Before reading this chapter try to answer the following question. The material is worked through in the text. Question and answers appear together at the end of the chapter by way of summary:

QUESTIONS

What are the objectives of marketing training?

What guidelines are helpful to a training programme?

What are the ingredients of a marketing training session?

What steps are involved in planning a training programme?

Chapter 9 synopsis

- How does training help?
- A useful structure
- Essential training ingredients
- How to train

HOW DOES TRAINING HELP?

Question What are the objectives of marketing training?

Marketing is a skill and can be learned. In professional firms marketing training sometimes brings with it both stress and irritation. The professional person who has achieved success and respect in his or her field has usually spent some years in practice and has developed confidence. Marketing activities are alien to such life experience. Worse, for many, marketing is tainted by the stigma of being intellectually undemanding or inferior.

Whilst a person of proven professional skill is clearly capable of mastering marketing skills, it may prove to be a tiresome exercise. Effort is necessary and the professional person, revelling in challenges to a finely honed professional skill, must exercise in a new field – an area without the experience of previous successes and solutions.

The task for the trainer – whether lecturer, managing director or marketing co-ordinator – is perhaps embellished with hostility and personal defence mechanisms.

The solution is to get the trainees to 'do'. In 85 per cent or more of an effective marketing training session, participants discuss, work in syndicates, work in pairs or alone, make presentations, evaluate or role-play marketing skills and techniques.

Training in marketing skills is a process of learning

about the marketing function. It is the process of adopting that function – and directing all professional and related practice activities to satisfying client needs.

A USEFUL STRUCTURE

Question **What guidelines are helpful to a training programme?**

A good trainer plans his or her training programme meticulously, and rehearses thoroughly before any training session. An experienced lecturer can go into the classroom without preparation, and cope on an *ad hoc* basis, but the results are not as good as when there is prior preparation.

A useful format for training seminars is as follows.

- Restrict class sizes to about fifteen participants. Larger sizes become unwieldy and learning achievement diminishes.
- The trainer gives a short introductory lecture. Visual aids such as overhead projector slides, flip charts, photographs or models are invaluable. Handouts are useful too, if they take away the need for the trainees to make notes whilst the lecturer is talking. If handouts are not provided the lecturer should allow time for salient facts to be copied. On no account should the session turn into a dictation period.
- Exercises are set for the participants to work through, for example prepare a checklist of dos and don'ts for writing and publishing a press announcement. The class is divided into small groups or syndicates. When each syndicate has reached a conclusion the class reassembles, and each syndicate presents its findings. The material

presented is recorded on a flip chart. Each person takes down the checklist items which will help him or her in the future.

- A commitment is obtained from each participant to behave or perform in a manner decided by the class as appropriate. A personal commitment to do something is a strong motivating force, and the person making it is likely to uphold it, at least for a short time. A word of caution, however: the commitment should be verbal and handled circumspectly. A written commitment may possibly be regarded as an infringement of individual rights, even though the peer group has decided on the format and extent of the commitment.

A fundamental principle of training practice is that trainees should *do*, rather than be *told*. If a participant in a training session works something out, he or she will remember it far more effectively then if he or she is merely told that it is so.

- Drip-feed training is more effective than total exposure training. Time constraints are a significant factor in a busy practice. Four two-hour sessions at weekly intervals achieve much greater learning retention than attendance at a one-day seminar. But training has to balance against practical considerations. A compromise of two half-day sessions is preferable to the single day.

ESSENTIAL TRAINING INGREDIENTS

Question **What are the ingredients of a training session?**

Marketing training has a twofold function: to gain the

participants' commitment to understanding and adopting the marketing function; and to develop and practise practical marketing skills.

First, the training aims are formulated. These come from the answers to the questions: where is the firm now? Where does the firm want to go? Where will the firm go without training? Objectives are then set to identify specific marketing targets. The ingredients of a training programme are a series of linked sessions. Each is designed so that the performance of participants can be measured against the set objectives.

HOW TO TRAIN

Question **What steps are involved in planning a training programme?**

The partners of a firm of consulting engineers decide that it is necessary to adopt the marketing function. A series of four half-day seminars is planned to introduce the marketing discipline and gain the commitment of the firm.

Marketing for the engineering profession

A series of four morning seminars has been arranged to introduce the marketing function and explore how marketing disciplines can contribute to progress. The programme is as follows.

Day 1	*The marketing function*
9.30–10.30	What is marketing? Controllable and uncontrollable variables of the marketing mix. How marketing helps the profession.

Coffee 10.45–12.30	*The marketing plan* How planning helps marketing. Preparation of a personal plan. Commitment.

Day 2 9.30–10.00	*The marketing function revisited* Review of success. The dos and don'ts of marketing.

10.00–11.00	*Marketing research* Sources in the UK and overseas. What to do with data. Building networks.

Coffee 11.15–12.30	*Presentational skills* How to make a presentation. The importance of visual aids. Addressing individual clients and addressing committees.

Day 3 9.30–10.00	*Thinking marketing* Marketing is a philosophy. How to remove traditional blinkers.

10.00–11.00	*Promoting the practice* Creating the right public image. Telling what we do. How the media helps. Using a design concept.

Coffee 11.15–12.30	*Negotiating contracts* The importance of preparation. Negotiation stages. The 'golden rules of bargaining'.

Day 4 9.30–10.00	*Marketing details* Dos and don'ts of marketing. Putting the client first.

10.00–11.00	*Practice development* How to win more contracts. Making clients seek your skills.

Coffee 11.15–12.30	*Manipulating the purchase decision process* How buyers think. Selling with dignity.

The planning steps of the programme are described in turn below.

Set objectives for the programme

Note that in this example detailed consideration is given only to the first session of the programme shown above. The objectives are going to reflect everything that participants try to achieve, how they set about their task and what they need to know. Appropriate objectives are formulated so that, by the end of the seminar, participants are able:

- to describe the marketing function;
- to identify and describe controllable and uncontrollable marketing variables of their engineering practice;
- to explain how the marketing discipline requires the commitment and participation of all members of the practice;
- to develop and implement a personal marketing plan.

Once the objectives are set, it is possible to identify the resources which are needed. Specialist trainers, if required, must be booked. A venue has also to be booked and appropriate materials ordered. The precise sequence of events following the setting of objectives is not significant. It is best to book the venue as early as possible, unless the firm's facilities are such that there are no problems. The next step is to arrange the venue.

Arrange venue

Book the training room for the period required. Itemize the equipment and resources needed.

- Tables with ten chairs arranged in U-shape
- Lecturer's table and chair at the opening of the U but with space between to allow the lecturer to walk into the U-shaped area
- Overhead slide projector
- Low table to support slide projector
- Screen
- Paper
- Nameplate stands
- Folders for handout notes
- Pens
- Water beakers and glasses
- Flip chart and felt-tip crayons
- Surplus chairs and table to accommodate casual visitors
- Wastepaper baskets

In addition, for sessions 2, 3 and 4 where practical skills are developed and practised, the following items are appropriate:

- Video camera/recorder/monitor
- Table to support monitor

The item 'wastepaper baskets' is important; in hired accommodation it is often overlooked. Surplus paper in the form of excess printed handouts, or wrappings, is usually a problem. The lecturer's table must never become cluttered. It impedes the smooth flow of the session if notes or overhead slides are buried beneath a mound of paper.

Figure 9.1 illustrates a convenient classroom layout.

It is useful to give participants on a training programme as much advance warning as possible, so that they can make suitable arrangements regarding absence from normal duties.

When the seminar programme is structured in advance, there is an opportunity for participants to think

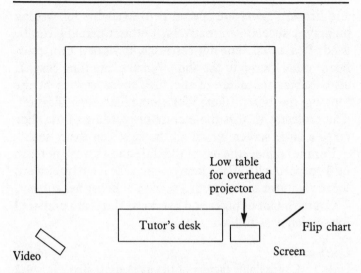

Figure 9.1 Training classroom layout

about the subject. With experience trainers can write a programme giving precise times of sessions, and then develop sessional material to fit the allocated time.

Notify persons who must attend the seminar of venue, time and programme

A memo is sent to all persons nominated to attend giving appropriate details.

Design course material

When all the peripheral activities have been dealt with, the course material is designed. The two most important requirements are overhead projector slides and course handout notes. Overhead slide projectors can be hired or purchased if not already owned by the firm. The slide is approximately 25x25cm and is an acrylic, transparent sheet on which designs, charts or wording are printed and drawn. There are special pens available for writing on acrylic sheets. Alternatively, Letraset printing can be used. It is usual, but not essential, to have a thin cardboard outer frame to the slide to make handling easy. It also enables the name of the slide to be written at the top, on the outer frame, for immediate identification. The projector throws the picture or wording of the slide on to a large screen which all the class can easily see.

For the trainer, the use of the slide allows work notes to be dispensed with. Each item on the slide is a trigger word for the lecturer to deal with a section of his or her subject.

Course handout notes and overhead slides are prepared for session 1 as follows:

Overhead slides		*Figure*
Slide 1	Controllable factors of the marketing mix: four Ps and an S	1.2
2	Controllable and uncontrollable variables of the marketing mix	1.5
3	Preparing the marketing plan	5.1

Handout notes		
Handout 1	Prompt sheet	9.2
2	Course objectives	9.3
3	Controllable factors of the marketing mix: four Ps and an S (photocopy of overhead slide)	1.2
4	Controllable and uncontrollable variables of the marketing mix (photocopy of overhead slide)	1.5
5	The marketing function: exercise	9.4
6	Preparing the marketing plan (photocopy of overhead slide)	5.1
7	Marketing plan exercise	9.5
8	Marketing plan: document 1: The plan	5.2
9	Marketing plan: document 2: Strategic analysis of the external environment	5.3
10	Marketing plan: document 3: Strategic analysis of the internal environment	5.4

11	Marketing plan: document 4: Awareness programme	5.5
12	Marketing plan: document 5: Communication activities	5.6
13	Marketing plan: document 6: Client service level improvement programme	5.7
14	Marketing plan: document 7: Client development programme	5.8
15	Marketing plan: document 8: Information system	5.9

Seminar format and procedure

As the participants arrive, invite them to sit anywhere at the U-shaped table. Each place setting has a folder, paper, pen, a blank name plate and handout 1, the prompt sheet (see Figure 9.2). Offer flip-chart crayons, which have a thick bold point, so that each person writes his or her name on the blank name plate. First names are always used in class.

At the beginning of this course, in turn with other participants, you are invited to stand up and introduce yourself. Saying who you are, and what you would like to get out of the course, allows the tutor to get to know his class. It helps everyone to settle into a comfortable working relationship.
The subjects you should cover are:

Name

Position in the company

How long you have been working in the company

Previous exposure to marketing

What you would like to learn from this course

Anything that causes you apprehension

Figure 9.2 Handout 1: Prompt sheet

---

1 Programme for introductory session

A very important contribution the first session makes to
the programme is to remove participants' apprehension
or hostility – and to settle everyone into a comfortable
working relationship. Although all participants are from
the same firm, they do not necessarily have more than a
casual relationship.

1.1 Handouts and slides are arranged neatly on the
     lecturer's desk. The person who is conducting the
     training introduces himself or herself.

1.2 Starting at one end of the table, participants are
     invited to stand up, in turn, and introduce them-
     selves. The prompt sheet handout is there for them
     to use if they wish. When they have said all they
     wish to say, or if they dry up, they just sit down.

1.3 Handout 2 is selected for distribution. Before
     giving it out, the lecturer says, 'Seminars and
     courses have to be about something; we cannot
     just chat indiscriminately. So I have written some
     objectives [see Figure 9.3]. It is our intention to
     meet these objectives by the end of the seminar.
     When I give them to you, please read the objectives
     carefully. Put a tick against the objectives which is
     most important for you, and a cross against the
     objective which is least important. Never mind
     what the person next to you does. When you have
     done this, I am going to go round the class and
     record on the flip chart those objectives which are
     the most important, and those which are least
     important. This is a good indication of how the
     class thinks.'

1.4 Distribute handout 2, Course objectives. Whilst
     the class are reading and marking their handouts,

By the end of the seminar participants are able to:

- describe the marketing function;
- identify and describe the controllable and uncontrollable marketing variables of their engineering practice;
- explain how the marketing discipline requires the commitment and participation of all members of the practice;
- develop and implement a personal marketing plan.

Figure 9.3 Handout 2: Course objectives

draw a vertical line down the centre of a flip-chart page. On the left-hand side write in capitals 'Most important'; on the right-hand side write 'Least important'; underline each. Preferably use different colours – the more colours that are used the more stimulating it is for the class.

Make sure the class have understood the instructions and, when they are ready, write on the flip-chart the numbers of the objectives selected as most and least important. Do this for each person. Comment on the similarity or divergence of opinion within the class.

1.5 Comment on the timetable. Each person has received a copy in the memorandum sent. If it has not been sent the timetable would be distributed as a handout. It is prudent to have a supply available.

Stress that the timetable is flexible. It is designed to cover the appropriate material, but if the class is involved in a fruitful session, it does not have to stop just because the timetable says so. What is important is that the objectives are achieved.

1.6 What is marketing? Ask the class for a definition. Obtain as many contributions as possible. Never tell a person that his or her answer is wrong. Say that it is only partly right and invite help from others. Help the group by asking the difference between marketing and selling.

Trace the history of the development of marketing from the selling concept through the product concept to marketing as it is known today. Give illustration to show how marketing initially applied to consumer products such as baked beans and soaps, and then moved on to being applied to motor cars and industrial products. Today marketing plays an integral part in the supply of services.

1.7 Display overhead slide 1, Controllable factors of the marketing mix. Acknowledge the contribution of Professor Jerome McCarthy in formulating the concept of the marketing mix of four Ps. Invite members of the class to define what each of the four Ps and an S represents, before giving an explanation. In this way the involvement of the class is secured. Distribute handout 3 which is a photocopy of the slide.

1.8 Invite the class to take a piece of paper. They have been given the variables in the control of the marketer: 'Write down the variables which are beyond control.' When all have stopped writing ask for answers. Write the uncontrollable variables on a flip chart.

1.9 Display slide 2, Controllable and uncontrollable variables of the marketing mix. Ask members of the class to comment on each variable. Distribute handout 4 – a photocopy of the slide.

1.10 Divide the class into syndicate groups of three or four. Distribute handout 5, The marketing functions exercise (see Figure 9.4). [*Note that the handout should include a reduced-size copy of handout 3 for easy reference.*]

The marketing function of a professional firm has three aspects:

- to identify the needs of clients and potential clients in their market segments;
- to produce, promote and supply service benefits to satisfy those needs;
- to generate profitable fee income.

In syndicate consider the following.

- Which of the 'four Ps and an S' (product, price, place, promotion and service) makes the most important contribution to the marketing function?
- What variation, if any, would you expect to find between the marketing function in the UK and in Malaysia?
- Engineering excellence attracts engineering contracts, not marketing hype. True or false?
- Marketing engineering services has been described as an orientation of the total firm towards the marketplace. The reality is that marketing is a PR manager with a different title. True or false?

Appoint a speaker to present your syndicate's conclusions to the group. Give reasons to support your answers.

Figure 9.4 Handout 5: The marketing function: Exercise

Tell the class they have twenty minutes to prepare their answers. When ready invite a response from each syndicate. Lead a discussion on each question so that the opinions of all are considered. At the end invite someone to summarize the consensus of opinion relating to the marketing of engineering services.

1.11   After coffee the class reassembles. Ask in how many ways a marketing plan contributes to the progress of the firm. Display slide 3, Preparing the marketing plan.

   Go round the class, asking each person in turn to explain and expand successive items on the slide. Distribute handout 6 – a photocopy of the slide.

1.12   There is now a marketing plan exercise: distribute handout 7 (see Figure 9.5).

   Explain that it is not the brief of this session for the group to develop a full marketing plan. However, real benefits are possible if participants prepare and commit themselves to a personal

---

Eight checklist documents, numbered 1 to 8 relating to the preparation of a marketing plan [these are handouts 8 to 15, figures 5.2 to 5.9] are distributed to all participants. Working singly or in pairs you are allocated one of the checklists to study. Your task is to relate the document to your firm: it has been developed in a general format. You are allowed fifteen minutes' preparation time.

You are then invited to present the amended document to the group for discussion and acceptance as a working document. The documents will subsequently be collected for future application.

Based on the checklist document you have amended, you are now invited to prepare a personal marketing plan. Provided that the prime marketing activities of your document are covered, you are free to commit your contribution to contingent areas more closely allied to your specific professional speciality or work.

Draw up your personal marketing plan on the flip-chart sheet provided, for ease of presentation to the group. Thirty minutes' presentation time is allowed for this task.

Figure 9.5 Handout 7: Marketing plan exercise

---

marketing plan. Distribute a flip-chart sheet and crayon to each person.

The session can continue till 1.00 pm if there is insufficient time.

1.13 After all the participants have presented their personal marketing plans, stress the importance of each person fulfilling his or her commitment.

Summarize the material covered in the session, and advise the time and date of seminar 2.

SUMMARY

Question   **What are the objectives of marketing training?**

Answer   The objectives of marketing training are to introduce participants to the marketing function, to provide understanding and familiarity with the discipline and to engender commitment.

Question   **What guidelines are helpful to a training programme?**

Answer   Good training practice makes participants *do* rather than listen – this reinforces learning. Classes of any size can be managed but learning achievement diminishes in classes of more than fifteen. Training presented in a series of sessions achieves greater learning than from a single longer exposure.

Question   **What are the ingredients of a marketing training session?**

Answer   Marketing training has a twofold function: understanding and acceptance of the marketing function; development and practice of marketing skills.

Question **What steps are involved in planning a marketing training programme?**

Answer The steps involved in planning a marketing training programme are:

- set objectives;
- arrange venue;
- notify persons who must attend the seminar of venue, time and programme;
- design course material;
- arrange seminar format and procedure.

Recommended reading

Cowell, Donald W., *The Marketing of Services*, Heinemann, 1984

Denney, Robert W., *How To Market Legal Services*, Van Nostrand Reinhold, 1984

Katz, Bernard, *How to Win More Business by Phone*, Business Books, 1983

Katz, Bernard, *How to Manage Customer Service*, Gower, 1987

Kennedy, Gavin, *Everything is Negotiable*, Business Books, 1982

Kennedy, G., Benson, J. and McMillan, J., *Managing Negotiations*, Business Books, 1980

Kotler, P. and Bloom, N., *Marketing Professional Services*, Prentice-Hall, 1984

Majaro, S., *Marketing in Perspective*, Allen & Unwin, 1982

Meidan, Arthur, *Insurance Marketing*, Graham Burn, 1984

Stapleton, J., *How to Prepare a Marketing Plan* (4th edition), Gower, 1988

Wilson, Aubrey, *Practice Development for Professional Firms*, McGraw Hill, 1984

Index